Coaching Youth Cricket

D0861238

Ian Pont

Human Kinetics

Library of Congress Cataloging-in-Publication Data

Pont, Ian.
  Coaching youth cricket / Ian Pont.
    p. cm.
  ISBN-13: 978-0-7360-8370-6 (soft cover)
  ISBN-10: 0-7360-8370-7 (soft cover)
  1. Cricket for children. I. Title.
  GV929.3.P66 2010
  796.35807'7--dc22
                                        2009053668
ISBN-10: 0-7360-8370-7 (print)
ISBN-13: 978-0-7360-8370-6 (print)

Copyright © 2010 by Human Kinetics, Inc.

This book is copyrighted under the Berne Convention. All rights are reserved. Apart from any fair dealing for the purposes of private study, research, criticism, or review, as permitted under the Copyright, Designs, and Patents Act 1988, no part of this publication may be reproduced, stored in a retrieval system, or transmitted in any form or by any means, electronic, electrical, chemical, mechanical, optical, photocopying, recording, or otherwise, without prior written permission of the publisher.

Notice: Permission to reproduce the following material is granted to instructors and agencies who have purchased *Coaching Youth Cricket:* pp. 160-165. The reproduction of other parts of this book is expressly forbidden by the above copyright notice. Persons or agencies who have not purchased *Coaching Youth Cricket* may not reproduce any material.

The Web addresses cited in this text were current as of February 2010, unless otherwise noted.

Acquisitions Editor: John Dickinson; **Developmental Editor:** Laura Floch; **Assistant Editor:** Elizabeth Evans; **Copyeditor:** John Wentworth; **Permission Manager:** Martha Gullo; **Graphic Designer:** Nancy Rasmus; **Graphic Artist:** Kim McFarland; **Cover Designer:** Keith Blomberg; **Photographer (cover):** iStockphoto/stuart hannagan; **Photographer (interior):** Nigel Farrow; **Visual Production Assistant:** Joyce Brumfield; **Photo Production Manager:** Jason Allen; **Art Manager:** Kelly Hendren; **Associate Art Manager:** Alan L. Wilborn; **Illustrator:** Tacklesport; **Printer:** Versa Press

We thank La Manga Club in La Manga, Murcia, Spain, for assistance in providing the location for the photo shoot for this book.

Games practices & skill drills included here were provided by Tacklesport (Consultancy) Ltd.; Animated Skill Drills for Cricket, republished as G.A.P.S. Cricket, Andrew Cushing; Year of publication: 1999, Copyright year: 1999, Republished: 2011, Worcester, UK. Tacklesport (Consultancy) Ltd.

Copies of this book are available at special discounts for bulk purchase for sales promotions, premiums, fund-raising, or educational use. Special editions or book excerpts can also be created to specifications. For details, contact the Special Sales Manager at Human Kinetics.

Printed in the United States of America   10   9   8   7   6   5   4   3   2

The paper in this book is certified under a sustainable forestry program.

Human Kinetics
Web site: www.HumanKinetics.com

United States: Human Kinetics, P.O. Box 5076, Champaign, IL 61825-5076
800-747-4457
e-mail: humank@hkusa.com

Canada: Human Kinetics, 475 Devonshire Road Unit 100, Windsor, ON N8Y 2L5
800-465-7301 (in Canada only)
e-mail: info@hkcanada.com

Europe: Human Kinetics, 107 Bradford Road, Stanningley, Leeds LS28 6AT, United Kingdom
+44 (0) 113 255 5665
e-mail: hk@hkeurope.com

Australia: Human Kinetics, 57A Price Avenue, Lower Mitcham, South Australia 5062
08 8372 0999
e-mail: info@hkaustralia.com

New Zealand: Human Kinetics, P.O. Box 80, Torrens Park, South Australia 5062
0800 222 062
e-mail: info@hknewzealand.com

E4848

Contents

Foreword

If I was asked what is the most important thing for a youth coach to be if they wanted to be successful, I would say, "to be encouraging." Because the truth is, if you do nothing else in your coaching career but encourage, you will have one of the best tools for bringing through any young cricketer.

Coaching isn't necessarily about finding fault or even correcting things you see. In fact it's easy to be critical. But coaching is rather about facilitating so a player can develop and evolve themselves with your guidance—and that's because the greatest gift you can give any player is one of self-awareness.

Whether you ultimately have a long career as a coach or not, you'll probably find that you can influence young players far more than older ones. And coaching at youth level can be one of the most rewarding things you'll ever do. You get a chance to start a player out on the road and be a big contributor to their enjoyment. It is, after all, this enjoyment of cricket that binds us all together.

Even though I made it into the ranks of International cricket, I started out as a junior like anyone else, getting coaching from enthusiastic coaches at school and club who influenced my development. It was their passion for cricket that helped me take the steps on the road and build a fire inside me for cricket. Whether you are a fully qualified coach, enthusiastic volunteer, or proud parent, there is a synergy and love of the game, which you'll need to get across in your coaching. So I would say to you this—make cricket fun and encourage young players to discover things for themselves by letting them make mistakes. It is by making those mistakes that they will learn. And it is by learning that they improve. This coaching ethos works well at all levels of coaching, right to the very top.

The author of this book, Ian Pont, is someone I have had the good fortune to work with while I was at Essex as a player and he was coaching there. Ian's style has always been one of challenging me as a player and getting to the answers in sometimes a different and unique way. This book is written in a similar thought-provoking way, which I urge you to read and enjoy. It's aimed at first-time coaches and those who want to get a grounding in how to teach the basics correctly.

Finally, coaches can be truly inspirational. And that starts with inspiring yourself. If you have energy, drive, enthusiasm and are fair-minded, you will have many of the attributes needed to bring through the next generation of youth cricketers. I can assure you there is no greater feeling for any coach than to witness those you work with becoming better players. That journey starts right here. Good luck and I wish you well—however far up the coaching ladder you climb.

Andy Flower
Director of Cricket
England and Wales Cricket Board

Acknowledgments

Our special thanks for contributions in this book go to the following:

Tacklesport
Phone: 0844 848 7030
E-mail: sales@tacklesport.com
Web: www.tacklesport.com

Martin Williamson
Executive Editor
CricInfo.com

Pitchvision.com

CricketEquipmentUSA.com

Also note that the coaching methods and styles are those approved by Mavericks Cricket Institute (MCI), founded by the author for the improvement of players and the development of cricket talent. MCI is an independent and world-respected coaching organisation committed to excellence as well as advanced coach education. For further information about the author or the coaching, please visit www.maverickscricket.com.

Introduction

This book is a guide and companion for those of you embarking on the road to coaching youth cricket. It has been written with you in mind. It's not meant to be a definitive guide but rather a series of well-organised ideas and suggestions you can apply right away and over the season to get your young players performing well.

Coaching Youth Cricket is based on the experiences of coaches as well as the thoughts of people in cricketing authorities, clubs, schools, counties, and international teams. Because the book is based on real experiences, it is a practical, no-nonsense guide including many tried and tested sessions, examples, games, drills, and coaching tips to help you avoid many of the coaching traps coaches can fall into.

We can only urge you to learn from other coaches and take ideas from those who have more experience and thus better knowledge. Many of the cricket drills are based on exercises that have worked for years but have been tweaked here to be more modern and relevant for young teams. If you have ideas of your own that might work well, don't be afraid to try them out.

Any good coach is always learning. Strive to be a coach that can take in new information and apply it to your programme. Be open minded. Share ideas with other coaches. Remember that no one—not even cricket authorities!—has the exclusivity of being right all the time. This is why it's important to remain flexible and to work with people to achieve your coaching goals. And your goal is, and as a youth coach always should be, to provide enjoyment for youths and bring through as many cricketers as possible. Without young cricketers, the game will die. I salute you as a youth cricket coach. Enjoy the experience.

You, a Youth Cricket Coach?

If you are like most junior, school, or club coaches, you have probably been recruited from the ranks of concerned parents, sport enthusiasts, or community volunteers and have had little or no formal instruction on how to coach. When the call came for coaches to assist with the local youth cricket team, you might have answered because you like children and enjoy cricket and perhaps wanted to be involved in a worthwhile community activity. You might have played, or still play, the game yourself or have a son or daughter who plays. Or perhaps you answered the call to coach because you have always loved giving young people guidance and support and saw coaching as an excellent opportunity to do so. Whatever it was that brought you here, welcome to youth cricket!

Let's start with the single most important thing about coaching—something too many coaches lose sight of once they get caught up with the job of doing well. Something so fundamental, it's worth making clear right at the outset. Coaching isn't about you. It's all about the ones you coach. Beware of the coaching trap of thinking you are more important than your players. You are here for them.

So let's begin by looking at your responsibilities and what's involved in being an effective coach. After that we will discuss what to do when your own child is on your team and look at five tools for being an effective coach.

Your Responsibilities as a Coach

Coaching at any level involves much more than creating a batting order or teaching your players how to field properly or bowl at the stumps.

Coaching involves accepting the tremendous responsibility of parents putting their children in your care. This responsibility can be daunting. As a youth cricket coach, you'll be called on to do the following:

1. *Provide a safe physical environment.*

   Playing cricket holds inherent risks, but as a coach you're responsible for regularly inspecting the practice and competition fields and equipment (see the facilities and equipment checklist in appendix A on p. 160). Assure players and parents that to reduce injury risk as much as possible children will learn the safest techniques and that you have an emergency action plan in place for when something unexpected occurs (see chapter 4).

2. *Communicate in a positive way.*

   As a coach you will have a lot to communicate. You'll communicate not only with your players and parents but also with coaching staff, umpires, administrators, scorers, and others. Communicate in a positive way that demonstrates you have the best interests of your players at heart (see chapter 2).

3. *Teach the fundamental skills of cricket within a fun environment.*

   When teaching fundamental skills to young athletes, keep in mind that cricket is a game and meant to be fun. Help all your players be the best they can be fundamentally while creating an enjoyable environment. We'll show you an innovative games approach to teaching and practicing the skills young players need to know—an approach that kids thoroughly enjoy (see chapter 5). Also, to help your players improve their skills, you must yourself have a sound understanding of batting, bowling, and fielding skills (see chapters 7 through 9).

4. *Teach the laws of cricket.*

   Introduce the basic laws of cricket and incorporate them into individual instruction (see chapter 3). Many laws can be taught during practice, including the LBW (leg before wicket) law, wides and no balls, limited overs, fielding laws, and how to run between the wickets. Plan to review the laws whenever an opportunity arises during practices. This is often the best way to help young players learn how they work.

5. *Direct players in competition.*

   This includes selecting your team, relating appropriately to umpires and opposing coaches and players, and making sound tactical decisions during games (see chapter 10). Remember that your focus is not on winning but on coaching your kids to compete well, do their best, improve their cricket skills, and strive to win within the laws. It doesn't matter if you win or lose—it's all about giving the kids a chance to have fun and do their best. You might remember from personal experience that a good teacher in your formative cricket years can go a very long way.

6. *Help your players become fit and value fitness for a lifetime.*

   Help your players become fit so they can play cricket safely and successfully. We also want your players to learn to become fit on their own, understand the value of fitness, and enjoy training. Don't make your players do push-ups or run laps for punishment. Make it fun for them to get fit for cricket; this will help them stay fit for a lifetime. Cricket has changed so dramatically from the 1970s and 1980s, when fitness was not high on the agenda. Today, modern cricket requires that players are fit and healthy and look after themselves. Once players enjoy the benefits of good health they want to retain them for life, not just for sport.

7. *Help young people develop character.*

   Character development includes learning, caring, being honest and respectful, and taking responsibility. These intangible qualities are no less important to teach than the skills of hitting the cricket ball and bowling fast. Teach these values by demonstrating and encouraging behaviours that express them. Also remember that players learn and benefit from camaraderie. Cricket is a game played by individuals on a team. Individuals get to have gladiatorial one-on-one battles yet must rely on others to ensure victory. This is something youngsters should learn early. Stress the importance of learning to back each other up, even when not directly involved in fielding the ball or receiving a throw. Also emphasise playing within the rules and showing respect for opponents and officials.

These are your responsibilities as a coach. Remember that every player is an individual. You have a responsibility to your young players during their formative years. You must provide a rounded environment in which every player has the opportunity to learn how to play the game without fear while having fun and enjoying their overall cricket experience.

Your players will look up to you as one more experienced than them, especially if you have played the game yourself. If you haven't, that's okay—you can learn along with your players. If you don't know much about the game or how to coach it, don't worry. Much of the game is logical and straightforward. If you're a beginner, simply go over the basics and help develop confidence in your youth cricketers.

If you start coaching with the view that your players' development and enjoyment are of primary importance, you have a chance of getting things right from the get-go. This type of coaching is called player centric. It places the player at the centre of everything you do—or should do. For

Coaching Tip
Think of how you would like to be coached if you were learning something new. This can help you understand how difficult some players find being coached in a certain way even while others respond to the instruction well. For example, some people learn best by watching a demonstration of a skill. Others do best by viewing a photograph or video clip. Others learn best through trial and error as they try to execute the skill themselves.

elite-level players, top coaches spend much of their time asking players what they want out of sessions, how they wish to progress, and how they can facilitate that for them. This style of coaching works well for this level of player. When coaching youth cricket, try to get your players to take responsibility for their own experiences as soon as they can. Naturally, you will have to guide them and advise them, cajole and nudge them. And at times you will have to communicate information in an authoritative way so they understand some things are not negotiable. But overall, help your players believe they are paving their own way and that your input is simply a guide.

The best coach a player can have is him- or herself. The coach should be the next best. Try to help your players overcome their dependence on you. They need to learn to take responsibility. Some players are unable to perform without their coach and may use you as an excuse for bad performances. Don't let this happen. Be a mentor and guide as needed, but also help your players learn to take responsibility and build character by understanding how much depends on them. They will respect you for helping them with this. Young people like to be treated like grown-ups.

People learn from making mistakes. As babies we fell down dozens of times when trying to walk, but this didn't stop us from trying again. No one ever says, "This baby is not a walker, forget it." Coaching cricket takes the same format: Kids learn by falling down. Always encourage your players to go out and get things wrong because they must not be afraid to "fall," or make mistakes. Tell them, "Make as many mistakes as you need to." Engrain this in the minds of your young players with the caveat, "Just don't keep making the *same* mistakes." You want your players to progress, learn, evolve, and finally walk on their own.

While we're on the subject of making mistakes, remember that young players will take what you say at face value most of the time. Very few will question your words, so be cautious in what you say because they will probably try it. Even if your advice is not 100 percent accurate, if you speak with conviction you can be inspirational to youth cricketers. This is, after all, what we seek—to inspire our players to become interested in, excited and passionate about, enchanted by, committed to, and smitten with the wonderful game of cricket. You should be too. As a coach you are taking the first steps in one of the most important and fun tasks you can embark on: helping the next generation enjoy the game we have come to love ourselves.

Coaching Your Own Child

Coaching becomes even more challenging when your child plays on the team you coach. Many coaches are parents, but the two roles should not be confused. As a parent, you are responsible only for yourself and your child, but as a coach you are responsible for the organisation, all the players on the team, and their parents. Because of this additional responsibility, your behaviour on the cricket pitch will likely differ from your behaviour at home, and your son or daughter may not understand why.

For example, imagine the confusion of a young lad who is the centre of his parents' attention at home but is barely noticed by his father (the coach) in the sport setting. Or consider the mixed signals received by a young player whose skill is constantly evaluated by a coach (who is also her mother) who otherwise rarely comments on her daughter's activities. You need to explain to your child your new responsibilities and how they may affect your relationship when coaching. Take the following steps to avoid problems when coaching your own child:

- Ask your child if he or she wants you to coach the team.
- Explain why you want to be involved with the team.
- Discuss with your child how your interactions will change when you take on the role of coach at practices or games.
- Limit your coaching behaviour to when you are in the coaching role.
- Avoid parenting during practice or game situations to keep your role clear in your child's mind.
- Reaffirm your love for your child, irrespective of his or her performance on the cricket field.

Coaching Tip

Discuss your interest in coaching the cricket team with your child before making a decision. If he or she has strong reservations about your taking over the head coaching job, consider becoming involved in a smaller role instead, such as being an assistant coach, serving as the scorer or umpire for the team, or organising a group of parents who provide drinks and snacks at practices and games.

Ideally, other parents watching a practice or a game should not be able to tell which player is the coach's son or daughter. You should treat all players equally and avoid singling your own child out in any way different from others on the team.

Five Tools of an Effective Coach

To be successful you'll need five tools that can't be bought. These tools are available only through self-examination and hard work. You can remember them by the acronym COACH:

C   Comprehension

O   Outlook

A   Affection

C   Character

H   Humour

Comprehension

You must comprehend the rules and skills of cricket and understand the basic elements of the sport. If you are new to cricket, here are some ways to improve your comprehension of the game:

- Study the rules in chapter 3 of this book.
- Read about the fundamental skills in chapters 7 through 9.
- Read additional cricket coaching books, including those available from your local or national cricket authority.
- Contact youth cricket organisations.
- Attend cricket coaching clinics.
- Talk with experienced coaches.
- Observe local school and youth cricket games.
- Watch cricket games on television.

In addition to having cricket knowledge, you must implement proper training and safety methods so your players can participate with little risk of injury. Even so, injuries may occur. And more often than not, you'll be the first person responding to your players' injuries, so be sure you understand the basic emergency care procedures described in chapter 4. Also, read in that chapter how to handle more serious sport injury situations.

Outlook

The second coaching tool refers to your perspective and goals—what you seek as a coach. The most common coaching objectives are to have fun; to help players develop their physical, mental, and social skills; and to strive to win. Thus your outlook involves your priorities, your planning, and your vision for the future. See Assessing Your Priorities for more on the priorities you set for yourself as a coach.

Here's a motto to help you keep your outlook in line with the best interests of the kids on your team. It summarises in four words all you need to remember when establishing your coaching priorities:

Players first, winning second

This motto recognises that striving to win is an important, even vital, part of sports. But it emphatically states that no efforts in striving to win should be made at the expense of the players' well-being, development, and enjoyment.

> **Coaching Tip**
> Local school games are a low-cost way to improve your knowledge of the game and also to allow players of all ages to see the technical and tactical skills they're working on in action. Consider working with your team's parents to organise a team outing to a local game in place of an after-school or weekend practice.

Assessing Your Priorities

Although all coaches focus on competition, we want you to focus on *positive* competition—keeping the pursuit of victory in perspective by making decisions that, first, are in the best interest of the players and, second, will help win the game.

So, how do you know if your outlook and priorities are in order? Here's a little test:

1. Which outcome would you be most proud of?
   a. *Knowing that each participant enjoyed playing cricket*
   b. *Seeing that all players improved their cricket skills*
   c. *Winning the competition*

2. Which statement best reflects your thoughts about sport?
   a. *If it isn't fun, don't do it.*
   b. *Everyone should learn something every day.*
   c. *Sport isn't fun if you don't win.*

3. How would you like your players to remember you?
   a. *As a coach who was fun to play for*
   b. *As a coach who provided a good base of fundamental skills*
   c. *As a coach who had a winning record*

4. Which would you most like to hear a parent of a player on your team say?
   a. *Nick really had a good time playing cricket this year.*
   b. *Nick learned some important lessons playing cricket this year.*
   c. *Nick played on the first eleven cricket team this year.*

5. Which of the following would be the most rewarding moment of your season?
   a. *Having your team want to continue playing, even after practice is over*
   b. *Seeing one of your players finally master the skill of fielding and throwing accurately to the stumps*
   c. *Winning the competition*

Look over your answers. If you most often selected "a," then having fun is most important to you. A majority of "b" answers suggests that skill development is what attracts you to coaching. And if "c" is your most frequent response, winning is tops on your list of coaching priorities, and perhaps you should think again. If your priorities are suitable for youth cricket, your players' well-being will take precedence over your team's win–loss record every time.

Take the following actions to better define your outlook:

- With your coaches, determine your priorities for the season.
- Prepare for situations that challenge your priorities.
- Set goals for yourself and your players that are consistent with your priorities.
- Plan how you and your players can best attain your goals.
- Review your goals frequently to be sure you are staying on track.

Affection

Another vital tool in your coaching kit is a genuine concern for the young people you coach. This requires having a passion for kids, a desire to share with them your enjoyment and knowledge of cricket, and the patience and understanding that allow each player to grow from their involvement in sport. You can demonstrate your affection and patience in many ways, including the following:

- Make an effort to get to know each player on your team.
- Treat each player as an individual.
- Empathise with players trying to learn new and difficult skills.
- Treat players as you would like to be treated under similar circumstances.
- Control your emotions.
- Show your enthusiasm for being involved with your team.
- Keep an upbeat tempo and a positive tone in all your communications.

Character

The fact that you have decided to coach youth cricket probably means you think participation in sport is important. But whether that participation develops character in your players depends as much on you as it does on the sport itself. How can you help your players build character?

Having good character means modelling appropriate behaviours for sport and life. This means more than just saying the right things. What you say and what you do must match. There is no place in coaching for a "Do as I say, not as I do" philosophy. Challenge, support, encourage, and reward every youngster, and your players will be more likely to accept, even celebrate, their differences. Be in control before, during, and after all practices and games. And don't be afraid to admit that you are wrong. No one is perfect!

Each member of your coaching staff should take the following steps toward becoming a good role model:

- Take stock of your strengths and weaknesses.
- Build on your strengths.

- Set goals for yourself to improve on those areas you don't want to see copied.
- If you slip up, apologise to your team and to yourself. You'll do better next time.

Humour

Humour is an often overlooked coaching tool. For our purposes, humour means having the ability to laugh at yourself and with your players during practices and games. Nothing helps balance the seriousness of a skill session like a chuckle or two. And a sense of humour puts in perspective the many mistakes your players will make. So don't get upset over each miscue or respond negatively to erring players. Allow yourself and your players to enjoy the ups without dwelling on the downs. Here are some tips for injecting humour into your practices:

- Make practices fun by including a variety of activities.
- Keep all players involved in games and skill practices.
- Consider laughter by your players a sign of enjoyment, not of waning discipline.
- Smile!

As an overview to coaching then, remember to deliver what you have to deliver with belief, fairness, and enjoyment. The game of cricket should be fun for all involved. A good coach should always be seeking ways of introducing new drills, better practices, and more interesting methods of practicing. Variety makes things more interesting for you as the coach and much more fun for your cricketers.

Whatever your reasons for wanting to coach, bear the tips and guidelines in this chapter in mind. Remember that we all look back with fondness on our great teachers. A really good coach can do wonders for a player. A great coach can perform minor miracles. That's why coaching can be so rewarding. You are embarking on the most important job you could choose.

Have fun, and make it fun for your players!

Coaching Tip

Younger players in particular are often nervous about meeting new people and starting a new activity. A good way to break the ice with younger age groups is to tell a joke at the beginning of the first few practices. Here are a couple of old standbys:

Q: Why did it get really hot after the cricket game?

A: All the fans went home!

Q: Why did the cricket player go to jail?

A: He got caught taking a quick single!

Communicating as a Coach

This chapter might be the most important in the book. The information here applies to all levels of coaching, from level 1 through level 4, and across all countries and cricket board certificates. The elements discussed are simply so fundamental to cricket that if you get them wrong, your career in coaching will be short-lived and probably unhappy for all involved.

First let's look at an all-too-common example of poor communication. A young player is batting particularly badly and not really doing what the coach has asked. The coach bellows down the lane to the player at the top of his voice, with three other full nets of coaches and players in easy hearing distance, plus a gallery of watching parents, "Son, you're wasting your time, my time, and your father's money." The boy is reduced to tears.

This is one of many such stories, far too many of them entirely true. To this day, those who heard that coach have not forgotten his comments. One can only wonder what happened to that young player, but if he ever fully recovered it would be a surprise. Clearly, there are far better ways of communicating. Being sarcastic toward children, belittling them, or making them feel ashamed in front of friends and family warrants an early and immediate end to a coaching career.

You can have fun with coaching kids and still remain professional. Actually, you must do this if you want to be taken seriously as a good coach. But consider the age of people you are working with and allow some latitude. If you have been a decent player, don't be surprised when others don't pick things up as quickly as you did in your career. Many former players come to coaching for the first time and end up being very poor coaches, not because they don't understand what they're doing but because they can't communicate what to do very well. This is sometimes a consequence of having been a natural rather than struggling to learn as a beginning player. In fact, history tells us that great players rarely make great coaches. Unfortunately, such coaches are often elevated in their players' eyes because of their name alone. Even so, some of them do not last very long.

Communication comes in many forms. Experience shows that coaches who understand and communicate effectively tend to make the best coaches. In chapter 1 you learned about the tools you need as a coach—comprehension, outlook, affection, character, and humour—all essential for effective coaching; without them, you'd have a difficult time getting started. But these tools don't work if you don't know how to use them with your players, and this requires skilful communication. In this chapter we'll examine what effective communication is and how you can become a better communicator. We'll look at methods of communicating clearly and effectively in different situations.

Communication in its simplest form involves two people: a sender and receiver. The sender transmits a message verbally, through facial expressions, or through body language. Once the message is sent, the receiver receives it and, we hope, understands it. A receiver who fails to attend to the message will miss part, if not all, of the message.

> **Coaching Tip**
>
> Some coaches mistakenly believe that communication occurs only when verbally instructing players to do something. In fact, verbal commands are but a small part of the communication process. More than half of communication occurs nonverbally. Particularly, remember when you are coaching that actions speak louder than words.

Sending Effective Messages

Young players often have little understanding of the rules and skills of cricket and probably even less confidence in their ability to play the game. This means they need accurate, understandable, and supportive messages to help them along. This is why your verbal and nonverbal messages are important.

Verbal Messages

The phrase "sticks and stones may break my bones, but words will never hurt me" isn't true. Spoken words can have a strong and long-lasting effect—much longer than sticks and stones, in fact. And coaches' words are particularly influential because youngsters place great importance on what coaches say. Perhaps you, like many former youth sport participants, have a difficult time remembering much of anything your elementary school teachers told you, but you still recall several specific things your coaches said. Such is the lasting effect of a coach's comments to a player.

Whether you are correcting misbehaviour, teaching a player how to hit the ball, or praising a player for good effort, strive to achieve these objectives when sending a message verbally:

- Be positive and honest.
- Speak clearly and simply.
- Say it loud enough, and then say it again.
- Be consistent.

Be Positive and Honest

Nothing turns people off like hearing someone nag all the time, and players react similarly to a coach who constantly gripes. Kids particularly need encouragement because they often doubt their ability to perform in a sport. So look for and tell your players what they did well.

However, don't cover up poor or incorrect play with rosy words of praise. Kids know all too well when they've erred, and no cheerfully expressed cliché can undo their mistakes. If you fail to acknowledge players' errors, your players will think you are a phony.

An effective way to correct a performance error is first to point out the part of the skill that the player performed correctly. Then explain, in a positive manner, the error the player made, and show him or her the correct way to do it. Finish by encouraging the player and emphasising the correct performance. This is the feedback sandwich you have heard about: helpful instruction sandwiched between two slices of encouragement.

Avoid following a positive statement with the word "but." For example, don't say, "That's well done stopping the ball, Barry, but if you use two hands next time, you'll be able to throw the ball more quickly." Kids tend to ignore the positive statement and focus on the negative one. Instead say, "That was a good stop and an accurate throw, Barry. And if you keep your throwing hand ready to take the ball when it comes into your hands, you'll be able to grab it even more quickly to throw it to the wicket keeper. Really well done."

Speak Clearly and Simply

Positive and honest messages are good only when expressed directly in ways your players understand. Beating around the bush is ineffective and inefficient. And if you ramble, your players will miss the point of your message and probably lose interest. Here are tips for saying things clearly and simply:

- Organise your thoughts before speaking to your players.
- Know your subject as completely as possible.
- Explain things thoroughly, but don't bore your players with long-winded monologues.
- Use language your players can understand, and be consistent in your terminology.
- Avoid trying to be hip by using their age group's slang.

Say It Loud Enough, Then Say It Again

Talk to your team in a voice that all members can hear. A crisp, vigorous voice commands attention and respect; garbled and weak speech is tuned out. It's okay and, in fact, appropriate to soften your voice when speaking to a player individually about a personal problem. But most of the time your messages will be for all your players to hear, so make sure to belt them out! An enthusiastic voice motivates players and tells them you enjoy being their coach. Some words of caution, however, about overdoing a good thing: Avoid dominating the setting with a booming voice that distracts players' attention from their performances.

Sometimes what you say, even if stated loudly and clearly, won't sink in the first time. This is particularly true when young players hear words they don't understand. To avoid boring repetition and still get your message across, say the same thing in a slightly different way. For instance, when an opposing batsman is looking for quick singles, you might first tell your players, "Okay, let's get the nonstriker!" If they don't appear to understand, you might say, "On a ball to the infield, throw at the bowler's stumps quickly for the run out. Don't allow the nonstriking batsman to get back!" The second form of the message might get through to players who missed it the first time around.

Coaching Tip

Keep in mind that terms you are familiar with and understand might be completely foreign to your players, especially younger players or beginners. Adjust your vocabulary to match the age group. Although 12- to 14-year-olds usually understand terms such as "good areas" or "bowl to your field," 8- and 9-year-olds might be confused by this terminology. In some cases it's necessary to use demonstrations so players can "see" the term and how it relates to the game of cricket.

Be Consistent

People often say things in ways that imply a different message. For example, a touch of sarcasm added to "well done!" sends an entirely different message than the words themselves suggest. Avoid sending mixed messages. Keep the tone of your voice consistent with the words you use. Don't say something one day and contradict it the next; players will get their wires crossed.

Keep your terminology consistent. Many cricket terms describe the same or similar skills. Take spin bowling, for example. One coach might use the term "off spin" to indicate turning the ball into a right-handed batsman, and another coach might say "off break." Both are correct, but to be consistent as a staff agree on all terms before the start of the season and then stick with them.

Nonverbal Messages

Just as you should be consistent in the tone of voice and words you use, you should also keep your verbal and nonverbal messages consistent. An extreme example of failing to do this is shaking your head, indicating disapproval, while at the same time telling a player, "well tried." Which is the player to believe, your gesture or your words?

Messages can be sent nonverbally in several ways. Facial expressions and body language are just two of the more obvious forms of nonverbal signals that can help you when you coach. Keep in mind that as a coach you need to be a teacher first; avoid any action that detracts from the message you are trying to convey.

To be a good coach, you need to be enthusiastic. This is a given. You cannot be a misery and enjoy great success coaching children. They will leave you in droves, and their parents will also desert you for a happier, more charming, and enthusiastic counterpart. Yes, there will be days when you don't feel like being enthusiastic, but do your best to conceal this until you can be genuinely upbeat again. If your players detect a lack of enthusiasm on your part, your coaching popularity will go downhill faster than a ferret on a toboggan. If you find that on more days than not, you can't muster enthusiasm for what you're doing, it's probably time to hang up your coaching shoes. You will be doing a massive disservice to your players if you have a general "glass half empty" attitude.

Facial Expressions

The look on a person's face is the quickest clue to what he or she thinks. Your players know this, so they will study your face, looking for a sign to tell them more than the words you say. Don't try to fool them by putting on a happy or blank mask. They'll see through it, and you'll lose credibility.

Serious, stone-faced expressions provide no cues to kids who want to know how they are performing. When they perceive such expressions, most kids will assume you're unhappy or disinterested. Don't be afraid to smile. A smile from a coach can give a great boost to an unsure player. A smile also lets your players know you are happy coaching them. But don't overdo it, or your players won't be able to tell when you are genuinely pleased by something they've done or when you are just putting on a smiling face.

Body Language

What would your players think you were feeling if you came to practice slouched over with your head down and shoulders slumped? That you were tired, bored, or unhappy? How about if you watched them during a contest with your hands on your hips, your jaws clenched, and your face reddened? That you were upset with them, disgusted by an umpire, or mad at a fan?

Coaching Tip

As a coach, be sure you are aware of your body language. Players of all ages will pick up on your actions and habits, so you must ensure that you provide a good example for your players to model. All it takes is a few eye-rolls or wild hand gestures to send a message that this type of behaviour is acceptable, even if that would never be your intent.

Probably all these possibilities would enter your players' minds. And none of these is the impression you want your players to have of you. That's why you should carry yourself in a pleasant, confident, and spirited manner.

Communication Breakdowns

Let's review some problems coaches can have when attempting to communicate. These are behaviours that you'll want to avoid for many reasons. Some involve sending mixed messages to young players, which can be confusing or unsettling for them. One example is saying one thing but doing another. As a coach, you must practice what you preach.

Young players expect to be treated fairly by their coach. For instance, be sure to communicate equally with all your players. Don't choose favourites, and don't put any player in your doghouse. A lack of proper team-wide communication can make some players feel undervalued, overlooked, or simply frightened and confused. Communication problems include but are not limited to these behaviours, all of which send the wrong message to your players:

- Not listening
- Assuming people have understood what you have said
- Not involving others
- Talking down to players, officials, or parents
- Taking sides
- Being rude
- Being dictatorial
- Losing your temper
- Not giving praise
- Being openly critical
- Being noncooperative
- Having favourites

This list applies to coaches at all levels but applies most critically to young players because they are far less reasonable and understanding when it comes to disappointment. When you are clear and concise in your communication, you can assist with the management of your young players' expectations. If players feel they cannot talk to you, for instance, or that you do not listen to them, their trust in you is compromised. Similarly, if you're unable to show empathy and understanding, young players might simply withdraw into themselves. You risk this by creating *any* kind of barrier. You want to keep all channels of communication open wide.

Physical contact is also an important use of body language. A high-five, a pat on the head, an arm around the shoulder, or a hand-shake are effective ways to show approval, concern, affection, and joy to your players. Youngsters are especially in need of this type of nonverbal message. Of course always stay within the obvious, appropriate moral and legal limits, but don't be reluctant to send a message that can be expressed only in that way.

Improving Receiving Skills

Now let's examine the other half of the communication process: receiving messages. Too often good senders are poor receivers of messages. As a coach of young players, you must be able to execute both effectively.

Regarding communication, receiving skills are often less developed than sending skills. People seem to enjoy hearing themselves talk more than they enjoy hearing others talk. But if you learn the keys to receiving messages and make a strong effort to use them with your players, you'll be surprised at what you've been missing.

Pay Attention

First, you must pay attention; you must want to hear what others want to communicate to you. That's not always easy when you're busy coaching and have many things competing for your attention. But in one-on-one or team meetings with players, you must focus on what they are telling you, both verbally and nonverbally. You might be amazed at the little signals you pick up. Your focused attention helps you not only catch every word your players say but also notice your players' moods and physical states. You can also get an idea of your players' feelings toward you and other players on the team.

Listen Carefully

How we receive messages from others, perhaps more than anything else we do, demonstrates how much we care for the sender and what that person has to tell us. If you care little for your players or have little regard for what they have to say, it will show in how you attend and listen to them. Check yourself. Do you find your mind wandering to what you are going to do after practice while one of your players is talking to you? Do you frequently have to ask your players, "What did you say?" If so, you need to work on your receiving mechanics of attending and listening. But perhaps the most critical question you should ask yourself, if you find that you're missing the messages your players send, is this: Do I care?

Providing Feedback

So far we've discussed separately the sending and receiving of messages. But we all know that senders and receivers switch roles several times during an interaction. One person initiates a communication by sending a message to another person, who then receives the message. The receiver then becomes the sender by responding to the person who sent the initial message. These verbal and nonverbal responses are called feedback.

> **Coaching Tip**
>
> Positive feedback can be verbal or nonverbal. Telling young players, especially in front of teammates, that they have performed well is a great way to boost their confidence. A pat on the back or a high-five communicates that you recognise a player's performance.

Your players will look to you for feedback all the time. They will want to know how you think they are performing, what you think of their ideas, and whether their efforts please you. You can respond in many different ways, and how you respond will strongly affect your players. They will react most favourably to positive feedback.

Praising players when they have performed or behaved well is an effective way to get them to repeat (or try to repeat) that behaviour. And positive feedback for effort is an especially effective way to motivate youngsters to work on difficult skills. So rather than shouting at and providing negative feedback to players who have made mistakes, try offering positive feedback and letting them know what they did correctly and how they can improve. Sometimes just the way you word feedback can make it more positive than negative. For example, instead of saying, "Don't throw the ball that way," you might say, "Throw the ball this way." Then your players can focus on what to do instead of what not to do.

Communication works both ways. If you can encourage a player to interact with you, you've achieved a huge step forward in helping them improve. But there will be times when you have to give negative feedback to your players. Sometimes you have reason to sit parents, players, or even your fellow coaches down and give them constructive criticism. How you do this is as important as the message itself. There's a real skill in maintaining respect and being firm but fair. Here are a few pointers:

Keep your emotions under control.

It's easy to say things you don't mean or will regret later if you are angry, upset, or out of control of your emotions. It's hard to remain balanced when you are emotional.

Speak in private, away from others.

We have all experienced lectures given to us within earshot of others who are not involved. No one wants to get negative feedback while others can hear what's going on. Sometimes speaking in front of others is unavoidable, but do so only when absolutely necessary. You can almost always find somewhere private to talk with someone, so be smart about it and don't create an atmosphere in which people are afraid to speak because it's not private. Respect the privacy of those you are talking with.

Focus on the action, not on the person.

When you criticise someone rather than what they did, you're asking for trouble. Focus on the behaviour or performance you want to change.

Be specific.

It does no good to tell someone, "You have a bad attitude." Identify specific actions the person took or specific things they said or did if you want them to understand you.

Seize the moment where you can.

Give negative feedback as soon as possible following the occurrence of the behaviour or performance you want to change. If you see a player being rude or disrespectful to others, pull him aside and tell him right away. Don't wait until the end of the game. How many others might they have offended in the meantime? Speak to your players immediately whenever possible.

Be calm.

It's a fact that in situations of perceived conflict people get stressed, angry, or upset. If *you* get like this, the person you're speaking to might not listen or might take what you're saying badly.

Back up your belief in the person.

It's important when giving negative feedback that you tell your players you still have faith in them and their abilities; it's only their performance you want them to change. Say things like, "You're a good cricketer, so I'm sure you see the need to be more open to improvement."

Keep quiet once you have spoken.

Speak, and then allow the other person a chance to respond to or refute your statements. Listen to what they have to say rather than fixing on what you are going to say next.

Define positive steps.

Agree on what future performance is appropriate. If players need to start or stop doing specific things, be sure the things are clearly identified. If there is something that needs to happen, such as additional training for a player, agree on that as well.

Move on.

After you have given negative feedback and agreed on a resolution, move on. Don't hold a grudge just because a player has made a mistake. Don't hover over her in fear she might make the mistake again. Monitor her performance as you do for all players, but don't overdo it.

Remember that this subject is covered in this chapter because many coaches have real trouble giving feedback (both negative and positive, to be honest) in a fair way. For example, some coaches create issues by being overly gushing or praiseworthy of a particular player in front of others, thereby constructing barriers among parents, players, and other coaches. Some coaches always seem to favour one player. Whether they truly do is hard to determine, but their praise for that player might be over the top and in full view or hearing range of other young players. Of course such behaviour looks and sounds unfair to others.

Children can get very jealous. Some believe that if someone else gets praise and they don't, it means they are not as good. There was an incident in which a coach was discussing a child's excellent cricket prospects with his parents, privately over dinner. That child had a best friend who was a highly skilled player and was coached by that same coach. Because the coach made his comments about only one player, the message came back that the coach didn't rate the other player (the best friend), who was far more advanced and already playing at a higher level. This little story shows that people are prone to pick up on comments, emotions, and subtle nuances involving other players, who are sometimes improperly viewed as rivals. Even the most innocent of comments intended to build a player's confidence can backfire on you, especially if taken out of context. Being (*and* seeming to be) fair-handed with players and their families is a difficult area for any coach. The key message here, then, is this: If you give praise, give it to all. If you give criticism, give it in private.

Communicating With Others

Coaching involves not only sending and receiving messages and providing proper feedback to players but also interacting with members of the staff, parents, fans, umpires, and opposing coaches. If you don't communicate effectively with these groups, your coaching career will be unpleasant and short-lived. Try the following suggestions for communicating with these groups.

Coaching Staff

Before you hold your first practice, meet with your coaching staff to discuss the roles and responsibilities each coach will undertake during the season. Depending on the number of assistant coaches, staff responsibilities might be divided into different areas. For example, one coach might be in charge of working with bowlers and wicket keepers, and another responsible for batters. The head coach has responsibility for all phases of the game, but, as much as possible, assistant coaches are responsible for their areas.

Before practices start, the coaching staff must also discuss and agree on terminology, plans for practices, schemes, game-day organisation, methods of communicating during practices and games, and game conditions. The coaches on your staff must present a united front and speak with one voice, and they must all take a similar approach to coaching, interacting with players and parents, and interacting with one another. Discussions or disagreements should be conducted away from the field, where each coach can have a say and the staff can come to an agreement.

Although it's important for all coaches to share similar coaching philosophies and be able to work together, you and your assistant coaches need not be identical. On the contrary, try to find assistant coaches who can complement areas where you aren't as strong. For example, perhaps you're confident in your ability to teach your players the fundamentals of fielding, bowling, and batting, but you're not very familiar with the nuances of the various types of deliveries, and you sometimes struggle with handling all the logistics of reserving practice times or notifying parents and players of last-minute schedule changes. In such a situation, consider recruiting an assistant coach who can take over the bowling responsibilities, and ask another assistant coach, or a parent, to help you manage the details of communicating game and practice schedules to the team.

Parents

A player's parents need to be assured that their son or daughter is under the direction of a coach who is both knowledgeable about the sport and concerned about their child's well-being. You can put their worries to rest by holding a preseason parent orientation meeting in which you describe your background and your approach to coaching. The type of paperwork needed before the season starts, as well as procedures and costs for handing out or purchasing equipment, will vary by team and league. See Preseason Meeting Topics (p. 22) for an outline of information to cover at a parent orientation meeting.

If parents contact you with a concern during the season, listen to them closely and try to offer positive responses. If you need to communicate with parents, catch them after a practice or game, give them a phone call, or send a note through e-mail or the mail. Messages sent to parents through players are too often lost, misinterpreted, or forgotten.

One of the biggest complaints from parents of up-and-coming players is that their children's coaches lack communication skills. It is true that for one reason or another many coaches fail to be understood clearly in the content of what they're saying, or sometimes don't even bother to explain things to players and parents. An entire chapter could be written on the complexities of dealing with parents. The politics of competitiveness and envy—why so-and-so's child hasn't been selected and why someone else's has been instead—can drive some coaches to shut down and stop communicating at all. But parents deserve clear messages about their children. If they want to be involved, that's usually a good thing.

Preseason Meeting Topics

1. Share your coaching philosophy.

2. Outline paperwork that is needed:
   - Copy of player's birth certificate
   - Completed player's application and payment record
   - Report card from previous year
   - Participation agreement form
   - Informed consent form
   - Emergency information card

3. Go over the inherent risks of cricket and other safety issues, and review your emergency action plan.

4. Inform parents of clothing and equipment procedures, including what items the league or team will provide and what equipment players must furnish themselves.

5. Review the season practice schedule, including date, location, and time of each practice.

6. Review proper gear and attire that should be worn at each practice session.

7. Discuss nutrition, hydration, and rest for players.

8. Explain goals for the team.

9. Cover methods of communication: e-mail list, emergency phone numbers, interactive Web site, and so on.

10. Discuss ways that parents can help with the team.

11. Discuss standards of conduct for coaches, players, and parents.

12. Provide time for questions and answers.

Much of the hassle in dealing with parents is caused by their lack of complete information about what's going on. This might be because they do not appreciate cricket to the levels you do, but more often it's because they feel they are being left out of the loop. So communicate with parents clearly and strive to have friends in the home of the children you coach.

Fans and Supporters

The boundary probably won't be overflowing with crowds at your contests, which means you'll more easily hear the few supporters who criticise your coaching. When you hear something negative about the job you're doing, don't respond. Keep calm, consider whether the message has any value, and, if not, forget it. Acknowledging critical, unwarranted comments from a fan during a contest only encourages others to voice their opinions. So fold down your rabbit ears and communicate to fans through your actions that you are a confident, competent coach.

Prepare your players for criticism from fans. Tell them it's you, not the spectators, they should listen to. If you notice that players are rattled by spectator comments, reassure them that your evaluation is more objective and favourable—and the one that counts.

Umpires

The way you communicate with umpires influences how your players behave toward them. Set an example. Greet umpires with a handshake, an introduction, and perhaps casual conversation about the upcoming contest. Indicate your respect for them before, during, and after the game. Never make nasty remarks, shout, or use disrespectful body gestures. Your players witness your actions and understand that such behaviour is appropriate.

Opposing Coaches

Try to visit with the coach of the opposing team before the game. During the game, don't be lured into personal feuds with the other team's coaches. Remember that it's the kids, not the coaches, who are competing. By getting along with the opposing coach and showing all due respect, you show your players that competition is all about cooperation and sportsmanship.

Communicating correctly can make a coach far more effective in getting the message across. Much of it is common sense, but it is worth understanding how *you* communicate and can improve on your skills, as being a better communicator will make your coaching easier. Spend time to review your skills in this area and don't be afraid to make changes.

3

Understanding Rules and Equipment

Y ou can't run a team or manage a junior side without knowing the rules and regulations of the sport you are coaching and the equipment your players will be using. In this chapter we'll first review the rules and regulations for junior cricket before turning to an overview on equipment for the sport.

Rules

Though the title of the chapter mentions rules, in the sport of cricket these are really called *laws.* Many of the laws of cricket are complex, so it's worth spending time to make sense of them. If you have played the game yourself you'll be familiar with the laws, at least most of them. Certainly you'll know the laws most relevant to the smooth running of a game. The more obscure laws will be known by an umpire (who must know them to become an umpire), so you can always ask if you're unsure.

We won't review all the laws of the game but only the basic ones that a youth cricket coach needs to know. To supplement the information in this chapter, your national or regional cricket board has excellent information sheets detailing the directives and guidelines you'll need to be familiar with to coach and manage youth cricketers. Find them by searching for your area's cricket board on the Internet.

ECB Recommendations for Junior Cricket

Conforming to the Laws of Cricket (2000 code) published by the Marylebone Cricket Club (MCC), let's consider some of the England and Wales Cricket Board's (ECB) recommendations for different age groups. Aspects such as size of the field, size of the ball, and type of stumps can be adjusted for various age groups to accommodate players' development and skill levels. Age groups are based on the age of the player at midnight on the 31st of August in the year preceding the current season, as shown below.

Age group	Type of ball	Ball size	Stumps*	Playing area
Under 7	Hard ball	4.75 oz	27 × 8 in.	16 yards (14.6 m)
	Soft ball	Kwik	Kwik	14 yards max (12.8 m)
Under 9	Hard ball	4.75 oz	27 × 8 in.	18 yards (16.4 m)
	Soft ball	Kwik	Kwik	15 yards (13.7 m)
Under 10	Hard ball	4.75 oz	27 × 8 in.	19 yards (17.3 m)
	Soft ball	Kwik	Kwik	16 yards (14.6 m)
Under 11	Hard ball	4.75 oz	27 × 8 in.	20 yards (18.2 m)
	Soft ball	Kwik	Kwik	16 yards (14.6 m)
Under 12	Hard ball	4.75 oz	27 × 8 in.	21 yards (19.2 m)
	Soft ball	Inter cricket	Inter cricket	20 yards max (18.2 m)
Under 13	Hard ball	4.75 oz	27 × 8 in.	21 yards (19.2 m)
	Soft ball	Inter cricket	Inter cricket	21 yards max (19.2 m)
Under 14	Hard ball	5.0-5.5 oz	28 × 9 in.	22 yards (20.1 m)
	Soft ball	Inter cricket	Inter cricket	22 yards (20.1 m)
Under 15	Hard ball	5.0-5.5 oz	28 × 9 in.	22 yards (20.1 m)

*27 × 8 inches = .68 × .20 metres; 28 × 9 inches = .71 × .22 metres

Adapted from The England and Wales Cricket Board, n.d., ECB recommendations for junior cricket. [Online]. Available: http://www.ecb.co.uk/ecb/directives-guidelines/ecb-recommendations-for-junior-cricket,501,BP.html [February 22, 2010].

ECB Fast Bowling Match Directives

The ECB has directives regarding the maximum age, maximum overs in a spell, and maximum overs in a day for fast bowlers in youth cricket. These are shown as follows:

Up to 13	4 overs per spell; 8 overs per day
Under 14 and under 15	5 overs per spell; 10 overs per day
Under 16 and under 17	6 overs per spell; 18 overs per day
Under 18 and under 19	7 overs per spell; 21 overs per day

Note that a fast bowler is a player whom a wicket keeper would stand back to take the ball. After completing a spell, the bowler cannot bowl again until the equivalent number of overs to the length of the spell have been bowled from the same end. A bowler can change ends without concluding a current spell as long as he or she bowls the next over that can legally be bowled from the other end. If this does not happen, the spell is ruled as completed.

Any spell in progress at the time of an interruption lasting for less than 40 minutes may be continued after the interruption up to the maximum number of overs per spell. If the spell is not continued after the interruption, the bowler cannot bowl again, from either end, until the number of overs equivalent to the length of his or her spell before the interruption have been bowled from the same end. If an interruption is 40 minutes or longer, whether scheduled or not, the bowler can begin a new spell immediately.

Once bowlers have bowled in a match, they cannot exceed the maximum number of overs per day even if they subsequently bowl spin. They can exceed the maximum overs per spell if bowling spin but cannot then revert to bowling fast until a number of overs equivalent to the length of the spell have been bowled from the same end. If they bowl spin without exceeding the maximum number of overs in a spell, the maximum will apply as soon as they revert to bowling fast. Captains, team managers, and umpires must follow these directives at all times.

Adapted from The England and Wales Cricket Board, n.d., ECB fast bowling match directives. [Online]. Available: http://static.ecb.co.uk/files/fastbowling2009-10462.pdf [February 22, 2010].

ECB Fielding Regulations

Following are the ECB regulations covering the minimum fielding distances for youth players in all matches in which a hard ball is used.

Players younger than 15 are not allowed to field closer than 7.3 metres (8 yards) from the middle stump, except behind the wicket on the off side, until the batsman has played at the ball. For players younger than 13, the distance is 10 metres (11 yards). These minimum distances apply even if the player is wearing a helmet. If a young player in any of these age groups comes within the restricted distance, the umpire must stop the game and instruct the fielder to move back. Any player under age 18 must wear a helmet and, for boys, an abdominal cup when fielding within 5.5 metres (6 yards) of the bat, except behind the wicket on the off side. Players should wear protective equipment whenever they field in a position that involves risk. These fielding regulations apply to all cricket matches in England and Wales.

Adapted from The England and Wales Cricket Board, n.d., Fielding regulations. [Online]. Available: http://static.ecb.co.uk/files/fieldingregulations2009-10464.pdf [February 22, 2010].

ECB Guidelines for Junior Cricketers in Adult Matches

The following guidelines apply to young cricketers participating in adult matches. Again, age groups are based on the age of the player at midnight on the 31st of August in the year preceding the current season.

All clubs are responsible for the safety of all players who are representing the club. This duty of care extends to leagues that allow young players to participate in adult teams in their league. The duty of care has two interpretations: (1) Do not place a player in a position of unreasonable risk (that is, clubs must take account of the circumstances of the match and the relative skills of the player); and (2) do not create a situation that places members of the opposing side in a position in which they cannot play cricket as they would normally against adult players. In addition, the following requirements apply to young players in adult matches: All young players younger than 18 years of age must wear a helmet with a face guard when batting and when standing up to the stumps when keeping wicket. Parental consent not to wear a helmet is not accepted in adult matches. A young player functioning as a runner must also wear a helmet, even if the player being run for is not doing so.

Umpires and captains must adhere to the current ECB fielding regulations. The umpires have the authority to stop the game immediately if a young player comes within the restricted distance. The umpires and the opposing captain must be notified of any players under age 19 participating in an adult match, even if the player is not a fast bowler. This requirement also applies to any young player taking the field as a substitute fielder. The ECB team sheet cards are available to facilitate this.

Before participating in adult matches, any player age 13 or younger must have the written consent of a parent or guardian. Clubs must ensure that they obtain parental consent and that this requirement is clearly stated in their registration procedures. Players must adhere to guidelines regarding changing and showering (see Safe Hands—Cricket's Policy for Safeguarding Children, which can be found on the ECB web site, www.ecb.co.uk). Any club wishing to use a player in the under-11 age group in an adult league or cup match must obtain the explicit consent of the league or cup management before the player can play. They should grant approval only to exceptionally talented players. Advice should be sought from the county age group coach or other ECB level 3 coach, as appropriate. Clubs and leagues can use their own discretion in applying more rigid restrictions on the participation of young players in adult matches. A parent, guardian, or other appointed adult should be present whenever a player in the under-13 age group or younger plays in an adult match. For example, the captain or other adult player could assume responsibility for the young player. This guidance applies to all cricket in England and Wales from the beginning of the 2007 season.

Adapted from The England and Wales Cricket Board, n.d., Junior players playing in Open Age matches. [Online]. Available: http://static.ecb.co.uk/files/juniorcricketers2009-10465.pdf [February 22, 2010].

Equipment

In cricket today, players are kitted out with great protection against injury, sometimes looking as if they're wearing a modern version of a suit of armour when they come out to bat. And there is good reason for this. Young cricketers must be protected from getting injured by the ball. Accidents and injuries in cricket are going to happen, but being unsuitably attired to avoid injuries or simply wearing inadequate protection should not be tolerated. As coach, you must ensure the safety of your players, so insist that they dress correctly. Protective equipment and clothing come in a variety of forms, so check your players regularly to make sure they're up to code. In the remaining sections of the chapter we'll discuss specific kinds of equipment and their guidelines for use.

Helmet

All young players must wear helmets. This law is now strictly enforced because over the years cricket balls have caused some very severe injuries. Never allow a young player to bat or keep wicket without wearing a helmet.

In February 2000, the ECB issued safety guidelines on the use of helmets by players ages 18 and younger:

- Players should wear helmets with face guards or grilles when they bat against a hard cricket ball in matches and in practice sessions.
- Young players should consider a helmet with a face guard, along with pads and gloves, as a normal item of protective equipment. Boys should consider an abdominal protector (protective cup) a normal piece of equipment.
- Young wicket keepers should wear helmets with face guards when standing up to the stumps.

Young players' use of helmets is now standard practice in cricket schools, clubs, and leagues throughout England and Wales. Helmets are widely available and are covered by a British Standard (BS7928:1998).

A helmet should have a good, snug fit so that it can absorb shock and minimize head injury. A helmet also needs to be lightweight. It should be made of a comfortable, absorbent material and allow air flow. A properly fitted helmet is worn with the peak protruding horizontally from the line of a batsman's eyebrows. It should feel firm but comfortable. There should be no excessive or unwanted movement in any direction to disturb the batsman. Batsmen should always fasten their chin straps for added security.

To measure a helmet for proper fit, run a tape measure just above the eyebrows, around the middle of the forehead, and around the side (slightly above the ears to the bump on the back of the head). Over time, the internal padding of a helmet will conform to the shape of the wearer's head.

Adapted from The England and Wales Cricket Board, n.d., ECB safety guidance on the wearing of cricket helmets by young players. [Online]. Available: http://static.ecb.co.uk/files/safetyguidance2009-10463.pdf [February 22, 2010].

Bat

Only the highest grades of willow produce the finest quality cricket bats. The world's best raw materials are needed for manufacturing excellent willows. Cricket bat willow is primarily sourced from the UK and Kashmir. Willows grow to a maximum height of about 21 to 27 metres (about 70 to 90 feet). The diameter is about .9 to 1.2 metres (about 3 to 4 feet). Trees grown for making cricket bats are felled after reaching a circumference of roughly 1.4 metres (about 4.6 feet). The density of the wood and the consistency of the grain right through a cricket bat's playing area is critical to the end balance and its performance.

Coaching Tip

The grain of the bat is important to its function—a detail often overlooked by people who buy bats. A bat with narrow grains will sometimes be slightly harder wood and thus last longer. A bat with fewer grains tends to be softer and feel as if it "goes" a bit better. There's always a trade-off for any player in choosing a bat that lasts or a bat that goes.

Getting the correct size bat is essential for the development of budding cricketers. The bat must not be too long or too heavy so that technique and stroke play are not compromised. Young players often use borrowed bats that are far too big for them, which means they are unable to defend themselves properly. Ensure the bat handle comes to the top of the player's thigh and that he or she has no problem making a proper backswing to control the bat. What you don't want is players losing control of their shots or, worse, the bat controlling what they do because it is too heavy.

Junior bats are proportionately scaled down in weight and size to meet this important requirement. Heavier bats usually result in a slower bat speed than lighter ones. A greater effort is also needed to use the heavy bat, whereas a lighter bat can yield faster bat speed and allows batsmen to have a better control of the bat.

The size and weight of the bat a player uses depends on the size of the player, his or her strength, and how comfortable he or she feels using it. Table 3.1 is a guide to choosing the initial bat size for a player determined by height.

Table 3.1   Bat Sizes Based on Player's Height

Height	Bat size
1.70 m and over	Full size
1.63 to 1.70 m	Harrow
1.57 to 1.63 m	Size 6
1.50 to 1.57 m	Size 5
1.44 to 1.50 m	Size 4
1.37 to 1.44 m	Size 3
1.29 to 1.37 m	Size 2
1.22 to 1.29 m	Size 1
Under 1.22 m to 1.22 m	Size 0

Batting Gloves

Batting gloves protect your players' fingers from injury. Batting gloves should fit snug but allow players to open and close their hands normally. Gloves must have adequate impact protection, especially on the thumb and fingers area. Each finger of both batting gloves and the thumb of the bottom hand (left hand for a left-handed batter and right hand for a right-handed batter) should have flexible padded areas for extra protection. Note that the critical measurement is from the beginning of the wrist to the longest finger's tip, in a straight line. This should ensure that the whole glove feels comfortable, allowing for wrist area, finger length, and palm width. The best way to measure is to try the glove on for comfort and check that all areas of the back of the fingers and thumb are adequately protected.

Batting Pads

Batting pads are important for young players because they protect the legs. Early beginners might opt to borrow pads from a teammate, but if they stick with the game, they will eventually need to buy them.

Batting pads should fit in a way that allows players to run naturally. The protection of the pads should cover the sides of the legs and be shaped to fit without sticking out. Straps, if there are any, should be tucked in so the ball doesn't hit them. Perhaps the most critical measurement to consider when wearing a pair of pads is the approximate distance down to the instep (where the tongue of the shoe would rest) from the middle of the knee cap. Pads are available in many sizes to suit different players but tend to vary slightly from one brand to another.

Wearing thigh pads is vital if you want to encourage your players to get behind the ball. The pad covers the region above the batting pad and up to the hip area, offering protection and allowing players to play with confidence. Once young players take a nasty, stinging hit to an unpadded thigh, they tend to lose interest in batting. As players get older they might also choose to wear an inside leg thigh pad that protects the inside of the back leg. Many a painful bruise has been avoided by wearing an inside thigh pad.

The abdominal protector, or box, is worn at all times by batsmen and wicket keepers. Taking a hit in the groin area is at best unpleasant. It's baffling to adults who play the game that anyone would attempt to bat without a box. Yet some do. There might be some embarrassment for a young player when first wearing one, but that's nothing compared to the pain of being hit. After a few games, a box is as natural to wear as a set of pads.

Wicket-Keeping Gloves

In a game of cricket it is not easy to find a substitute player for the wicket keeper from the playing 11, which is exactly why it's critical to wear wicket-keeping gloves of the highest standard. A broken finger on the wicket keeper is one of the most serious risks on the cricket field. Even if no break occurs, a hard smack to the fingers can be very painful. As with batting gloves, the critical measurement on the wicket-keeper glove is from the beginning of the wrist to the longest finger's tip, in a straight line. Wicket keepers should try gloves on for comfort and check that all areas, fingers and palm, are adequately protected.

Wicket-Keeping Pads

A wicket keeper is inarguably the most active individual on the field. The keeper needs to watch each and every ball, take crucial catches, stop byes, effect stump-outs, and encourage team members. Wicket-keeping pads protect legs from painful blows. The best pads are designed with all the necessary protection for any level of play. It's necessary for wicket keepers to wear a pair of pads that fit their legs and aid smooth movement behind the stumps. Comfort and ease of use is the critical element. Check for the sturdiness of calf and ankle straps; you don't want them to feel flimsy when crouching. Wicket-keeping pads are worn far longer than batting pads so should be comfortable and well made for longevity.

Cricket Shoes

For smooth and precise foot movement for batsmen, bowlers, and fielders, the proper cricket shoe is critical. The most important details in a shoe are comfort and grip.

Players should select their cricket shoes depending on the surface they're playing on. As a coach, help them out with this. Spiked shoes are good for soft ground, and pimpled rubber soles are suitable for hard ground. You can also find a combination of the two types, with both spikes and pimples. Batsmen generally prefer shoes with sturdy spikes at the front for proper grip combined with rubber-treaded heels. Fast bowlers usually prefer shoes with spikes at the front and back along with good support around the ankle. In indoor net situations keep a lookout for players wearing street training shoes that are fashionable but offer little protection for the feet. Well-built training shoes, with a strong heel impact area, can significantly reduce injuries.

Most cricket shoe sizes at online stores are quoted in UK sizes. Over the last few years there has been clear improvement on the part of manufacturers in standardizing sizes. You can be confident in making the right choice of size for your cricket shoes based on your normal shoe size, but don't forget to account for a thicker sock.

Though you do not decide what your players choose to buy or wear, as coach you should have an understanding of all equipment so you can advise players as necessary. The more supportive and comfortable the clothing and equipment, the more likely your players will perform their best.

You have a duty to ensure players take to the field properly attired. This is good for discipline and team spirit and gives your team a sense of union. Among young players, positive team spirit can be highly infectious. Never underestimate the importance of looking good and making the best equipment and clothing available whenever possible.

4

Providing for Players' Safety

One of your players gets under a high-hit ball to make a great catch. He makes a last-minute dive backward and sideways to take a wonderful one-handed grab centimetres from the turf. The umpire raises his finger, but you stop cheering when you notice that your player is unable to get on his feet and seems to be in pain. What do you do?

No coach wants to see players get hurt, but despite precautions, injuries remain a reality of sport participation. As a coach you must be prepared to provide first aid when injuries occur and to protect yourself against unjustified lawsuits. Fortunately, coaches can implement many preventive measures to reduce injury risk. In this chapter we'll discuss steps you can take to prevent injuries, first aid and emergency responses for when injuries occur, and your legal responsibilities as a coach.

Game Plan for Safety

You can't prevent all injuries from happening, but you can take preventive measures that give your players the best possible chance for injury-free participation. In creating the safest possible environment for your players, we'll explore what you can do in these areas:

- Preseason physical examinations
- Physical conditioning
- Facilities and equipment inspection
- Player matchups and inherent risks
- Proper supervision and record keeping
- Environmental conditions

Preseason Physical Examinations

All players should have a physical examination before participating in cricket. The exam should address the most likely areas of medical concern and identify youngsters at high risk. We also suggest that you ask players' parents or guardians to sign a participation agreement form (discussed later in the chapter) and an informed consent form to allow their children to be treated in case of an emergency. For a sample, see the informed consent form in appendix A on page 162.

Physical Conditioning

Players need to be in or get in shape to play the game of cricket at the level expected. They must have adequate cardiorespiratory fitness and muscular fitness.

Cardiorespiratory fitness relates to the body's ability to use oxygen and fuels efficiently to power muscle contractions. As players get in better shape, their bodies are able to deliver oxygen more efficiently to fuel muscles and carry off carbon dioxide and other wastes. At times, cricket requires lots of running and exertion. Unfit youngsters often overextend in trying to keep up, which can result in light-headedness, nausea, fatigue, and potential injury.

Remember that your players' goals are to participate, learn, and have fun. With this in mind, you must keep your players active, attentive, and involved during every phase of practice. If you do, they will attain higher levels of cardiorespiratory fitness as the season progresses simply by taking part in practice. But always watch closely for signs of low cardiorespiratory fitness; don't let your players overdo it as they build their fitness levels. You might privately counsel youngsters who appear overly winded, suggesting that they train under proper supervision outside of practice to increase their fitness.

Muscular fitness encompasses strength, muscular endurance, power, speed, and flexibility. This type of fitness is affected by physical maturity as well as strength training and other types of training. Your players will likely exhibit a wide range of muscular fitness. Those who have greater muscular fitness will be able to run faster and throw harder. They'll also sustain fewer muscular injuries, and when injuries do occur they will tend to be minor. When they are injured, they will recover faster than those with lower levels of muscular fitness.

Two other components of fitness and injury prevention are the warm-up and the cool-down. Although young bodies are generally very limber, they can become tight through inactivity. In your

Coaching Tip

Younger players might not know when to break for water and rest, so you need to work breaks into your practice schedules. Also make water available at all times during the practice session. This way they can grab a drink when they need it and eliminate the need for long water breaks during practice.

warm-up address each muscle group and elevate the heart rate in preparation for strenuous activity. Players should warm up for 5 to 10 minutes doing a combination of light running, jumping, and stretching. As practice winds down, slow players' heart rates with an easy jog or walk. Then have players stretch for 5 minutes to help prevent tight muscles before the next practice or game.

Facilities and Equipment Inspection

Another way to prevent injuries is to regularly examine the field on which your players practice and play. Remove hazards, report conditions you cannot remedy, and request maintenance as necessary. If unsafe conditions exist, either make adaptations to prevent risk to your players' safety or stop the practice or game until safe conditions have been restored. You can also prevent injuries by checking the quality and fit of uniforms, practice attire, and any protective equipment your players use. Refer to the facilities and equipment checklist in appendix A (p. 160) to guide you in verifying that facilities and equipment are safe.

Player Matchups and Inherent Risks

We recommend grouping teams in two-year age increments if possible. You'll encounter fewer mismatches in physical maturation with narrow age ranges. Even so, two 12-year-old boys might differ by 27 kilograms (about 60 pounds) in weight, 30 centimetres (12 inches) in height, and three or four years in emotional and intellectual maturity. This presents dangers for the player who is less physically mature. Whenever possible, match players against opponents of similar size and physical maturity. Such an approach gives smaller, less mature youngsters a better chance to succeed and avoid injury while providing more mature players with a greater challenge. Closely supervise practices and games so that the more mature players do not put the less mature players at risk.

Although proper matching helps protect you from some liability concerns, you must also warn players of the inherent risks involved in playing cricket because failure to warn is one of the most successful arguments in lawsuits against coaches. Thoroughly explain the inherent risks of cricket, and make sure each player knows, understands, and appreciates those risks. Learn more about inherent risks by talking with your league administrators.

The preseason parent orientation meeting is a good opportunity to explain the risks of the sport to parents and players. It is also a good time to have players and their parents sign a participation agreement form or waiver releasing you from

Coaching Tip

If your players vary largely in size, have players of similar size bowl to each other during practices. This will help prevent bigger players from bowling the ball too hard to smaller, less mature players who might have trouble handling fast deliveries relative to their build or ability.

liability should an injury occur. Work with your league when creating these forms or waivers, and ask legal counsel to review them before presentation. These forms or waivers do not relieve you of responsibility for your players' well-being, but they are recommended by lawyers and might help you in the event of a lawsuit.

Proper Supervision and Record Keeping

To ensure players' safety, you must provide both general and specific supervision. General supervision means you are in the area of activity so you can see and hear what is happening. You should be

- on the field and in position to supervise your players even before the formal practice begins,
- immediately accessible to the activity and able to oversee the entire activity,
- alert to conditions that might be dangerous to players and ready to take action to protect players,
- able and prepared to react immediately and appropriately to emergencies, and
- present on the field until the last player has been picked up after the practice or game.

Specific supervision is the direct supervision of an activity during practice. For example, you should provide specific supervision when you teach new skills and continue to do so until your players understand the requirements of the activity, the risks involved, and their own ability to perform in light of these risks. You must also provide specific supervision when you notice players breaking rules or a change in the condition of your players. As a general rule, the more dangerous the activity, the more specific the supervision required. This suggests that more specific supervision is required with younger and less experienced players, and also for older players who are learning and practicing more dangerous skills, such as facing short-pitched deliveries, diving in the field, or taking high catches.

As part of your supervision duty, you are expected to foresee potentially dangerous situations and be positioned to prevent them. This requires that you know cricket well, especially the rules intended to provide for safety. Prohibit

Coaching Tip

Common sense tells us that it's easier to provide specific supervision to a smaller group of players, regardless of age. Enlist the help of assistant coaches to divide your team into smaller groups to ensure your players can practice in a safe environment. The more adults who can help supervise, the better the players can learn and perform the skills of cricket. Smaller groups also allow each coach to provide more direct feedback to players.

horseplay and hold training sessions only under safe weather conditions. These supervisory activities, performed consistently, make the play environment much safer for your players and help protect you from liability if a mishap occurs.

For further protection, keep records of your season plans, practice plans, and players' injuries. Season and practice plans come in handy when you need evidence that players have been taught certain skills, whereas accurate, detailed injury report forms offer protection against unfounded criticism and perhaps even legal action. Ask for these forms from your club, school, or county organisation (see p. 163 in appendix A for a sample injury report form, which might look nothing like the form you use but gives you an idea of the information an appropriate form should contain), and hold onto these records for several years so that an "old cricket injury" of a former player doesn't come back to haunt you.

Environmental Conditions

Most health problems caused by environmental factors are related to excessive heat or cold, although you should also consider other environmental factors such as severe weather and air pollution. Foresight about potential problems and effort to ensure adequate protection for your players will prevent most serious emergencies related to environmental conditions.

Heat

On hot, humid days the body has difficulty cooling itself. Because the air is already saturated with water vapour (humidity), sweat doesn't evaporate as easily. Therefore, body sweat is a less effective cooling agent, and the body retains extra heat. Hot, humid environments put players at risk of heat exhaustion and heatstroke (see more on these under Serious Injuries on pp. 46-47). And

Coaching Tip

Encourage players to drink plenty of water before, during, and after practice. Even a small amount of water loss can cause severe consequences in a young body's systems. The day doesn't have to be hot and humid for players to become dehydrated. Schedule regular water breaks. Don't wait for players to say they are thirsty because by the time they do they are long overdue for a drink.

if you think it's hot or humid, it's worse for the kids, not only because they're more active but because youths under the age of 12 have more difficulty regulating their body temperature than adults do. To provide for players' safety in hot or humid conditions, take the following preventive measures:

- Monitor weather conditions and adjust training sessions accordingly. Table 4.1 shows air temperatures and humidity percentages that can be hazardous.
- Acclimatize players to exercising in high heat and humidity. Players can adjust to high heat and humidity in 7 to 10 days. During this period,

hold practices at low to moderate activity levels, and give players fluid breaks every 20 minutes.

- Switch to light clothing. Players should wear shorts and white T-shirts.
- Identify and monitor players who are prone to heat illness, including players who are overweight, heavily muscled, or out of shape, or players who work excessively hard or have suffered previous heat illness. Closely monitor these players and give them fluid breaks every 15 to 20 minutes.
- Make sure players replace fluids lost through sweat. Encourage players to drink 17 to 20 ounces of fluid two to three hours before practices or games and 7 to 10 ounces every 20 minutes during practice and after practice. Afterward they should drink 16 to 24 ounces of fluid for every pound lost during exercise. Fluids such as water and sports drinks are preferable during games and practices.
- Replenish electrolytes, such as sodium (salt) and potassium, which are lost through sweat. The best way to replace these nutrients, and others such as carbohydrates (for energy) and protein (for muscle building), is by eating a balanced diet. Experts say that during the most intense training periods in the heat, additional salt intake might be helpful.

Table 4.1   Warm-Weather Precautions

Temperature (°C)	Humidity	Precautions
27-32 (80-90° F)	<70%	Monitor players prone to heat illness.
27-32 (80-90° F)	>70%	5-minute rest after 30 minutes of practice
32-38 (90-100° F)	<70%	5-minute rest after 30 minutes of practice
32-38 (90-100° F)	>70%	Short practices in evenings or early mornings

Cold

When a person is exposed to cold weather, body temperature starts to drop below normal. To counteract this reaction, the body shivers to create heat and reduces blood flow to the extremities to conserve heat in the core of the body. But no matter how effective its natural heating mechanism is, the body better withstands cold temperatures if it is prepared to handle them. To reduce the risk of cold-related illnesses, keep players active to maintain body heat and make sure they wear appropriate protective clothing.

Severe Weather

Severe weather refers to a host of potential dangers, including lightning storms, hail, and heavy rains. Lightning is of special concern because it can come up quickly and cause great harm, even death. For each 5-second count from the flash of lightning to the bang of thunder, lightning is one mile away. A count of 10 seconds means lightning is two miles away. A practice or competition should be stopped for the day if lightning is three miles away or closer (15 seconds or fewer from flash to bang). Your school, league, or state association might have additional rules for you to consider in severe weather.

Safe places in which to take cover when lightning strikes are fully enclosed metal vehicles with the windows up, enclosed buildings, and low ground (under cover of bushes, if possible). It's not safe to be near metal objects such as flagpoles, fences, light poles, or metal stands. Also avoid trees, water, and open fields.

The keys to handling severe weather are caution and prudence. Don't try to get that last 10 minutes of practice in if lightning is on the horizon. Don't continue to play in heavy rain. Many storms can strike quickly and violently. Respect the weather and play it safe.

Air Pollution

Poor air quality and smog can present real dangers to your players. Both short- and long-term lung damage is possible from participating in unsafe air. Although it's true that participating in clean air is not possible in many areas, restricting activity is recommended when the air-quality ratings are lower than moderate or when there is a smog alert. Your local health department or air-quality control board can inform you of the air-quality ratings for your area and when restricting activities is recommended.

Responding to Players' Injuries

No matter how thorough your prevention programme, injuries are going to occur. When injury does strike, chances are you will be the one in charge. The severity and nature of the injury determines how actively involved you'll be in treating it. But regardless of how seriously a player is hurt, it is your responsibility to know what steps to take. You must be prepared to take appropriate action and provide basic emergency care when an injury occurs.

Being Prepared

Being prepared to provide basic emergency care involves many things, including being trained in cardiopulmonary resuscitation (CPR) and first aid and having an emergency action plan.

CPR and First-Aid Training

All coaches should receive CPR and first-aid training from a nationally recognised organisation. If you are studying to be, or are already, a UKCC level coach, you will have to have received training in CPR. You should be certified based on a practical test and a written test of knowledge. CPR training should include paediatric and adult basic life support and obstructed airway procedures.

First-Aid Kit

A well-stocked first-aid kit includes the following:

- Antibacterial soap or wipes
- Arm sling
- Athletic tape—3.8 centimetres (1.5 inches) wide
- Bandage scissors
- Bandage strips—assorted sizes
- Blood spill kit
- Mobile phone
- Contact lens case
- Cotton swabs
- Elastic wraps of various widths
- Emergency blanket
- Latex-free examination gloves
- Eye patch
- Foam rubber of various thicknesses (up to 1.2 centimetres, or a half-inch)
- Insect sting kit
- List of emergency phone numbers
- Mirror
- Moleskin
- Nail clippers
- Oral thermometer
- Penlight
- Petroleum jelly
- Plastic bags for crushed ice
- Prewrap (underwrap for tape)
- Rescue breathing or CPR face mask
- Safety glasses (for first aiders)
- Safety pins
- Saline solution for eyes
- Sterile gauze pads—7.6- to 10.1-centimetre (3-inch and 4-inch) squares, preferably nonstick
- Sterile gauze rolls
- Sunscreen—sun protection factor (SPF) 30 or greater
- Tape adherent and tape remover
- Tongue depressors
- Tooth saver kit
- Triangular bandages
- Tweezers

Adapted, by permission, from M.J. Flegel, 2008, *Sport first aid*, 4th ed. (Champaign, IL: Human Kinetics), 20.

Emergency Plan

An emergency plan is the final step in being prepared to take appropriate action for serious injuries. The plan calls for three steps:

1. *Evaluate the injured player.*

   Use your CPR and first-aid training to guide you. Be sure to keep these certifications up to date. Practice your skills frequently to keep them fresh and ready to use if and when you need them.

2. *Call appropriate medical personnel.*

   If possible, delegate the responsibility of seeking medical help to another calm and responsible adult who attends all practices and games. Write out a list of emergency phone numbers, and keep it with you at practices and games. Include the following phone numbers:

   • Rescue unit

   • Hospital

   • Physician

   • Police

   • Fire department

   Take each player's emergency information to every practice and game (see an emergency information card in appendix A on p. 164). This information includes the person to contact in case of an emergency, what types of medications the player is using, what types of drugs the player is allergic to, and other pertinent information possibly needed in an emergency.

   Give the injured player's emergency response card to the person calling for emergency assistance. Having this information ready should help the contact person remain calm. After the emergency has been dealt with, you must complete an injury report form (see the sample in appendix A on p. 163) and keep it on file. Do this for every injury that occurs.

3. *Provide first aid.*

   If medical personnel are not on hand at the time of the injury, you should provide first-aid care to the extent of your qualifications. Although your CPR and first-aid training will guide you, also remember the following:

   • Do not move the injured player if the injury is to the head, neck, or back; if a large joint (ankle, knee, elbow, shoulder) is dislocated; or if the pelvis, a rib, or an arm or leg is fractured.

   • Calm the injured player and keep others away from him or her as much as possible.

   • Evaluate whether the player's breathing has stopped or is irregular; if necessary, clear the airway with your fingers.

- Administer artificial respiration if the player's breathing has stopped. Administer CPR if the player's heart has stopped (that is, if the player has no pulse).
- Remain with the player until medical personnel arrive.

Emergency Steps

It is important that you have a clear, well-rehearsed emergency action plan. You want to be sure you are prepared in case of an emergency because every second counts. Your emergency plan should follow this sequence:

1. Check the player's level of consciousness.
2. Ask a contact person to call medical personnel and the player's parents.
3. Send someone to wait for the rescue team and direct them to the injured player.
4. Assess the injury.
5. Administer first aid.
6. Assist emergency medical personnel in preparing the player for transportation to a medical facility.
7. Ask someone to go with the player if the parents are not available. This person should be responsible, calm, and familiar with the player. Assistant coaches or parents are best for this job.
8. Complete an injury report form while the incident is fresh in your mind (see p. 163 in appendix A).

Taking Appropriate Action

Proper CPR and first-aid training, a well-stocked first aid kit, and an emergency plan help prepare you to take action when an injury occurs. We mentioned in the previous section the importance of providing first aid to the extent of your qualifications. Don't "play doctor" with injuries; sort out minor injuries that you can treat from those that need medical attention. Let's now take a look at appropriate action for minor injuries and also for more serious injuries.

Minor Injuries

Although no injury seems minor to the person experiencing it, most injuries are neither life threatening nor severe enough to restrict participation. When minor injuries occur, you can take an active role in their initial treatment.

Scrapes and Cuts   When one of your players has an open wound, the first thing to do is put on a pair of disposable latex-free examination gloves (or some other effective blood barrier). Then follow these four steps:

1. Stop the bleeding by applying direct pressure with a clean dressing to the wound and elevating it. The player might be able to apply this pressure while you put on your gloves. Do not remove the dressing if it becomes soaked with blood. Instead, place an additional dressing on top of the one already in place. If bleeding continues, elevate the injured area above the heart and maintain pressure.

2. Once the bleeding is controlled, cleanse the wound thoroughly. A good rinsing with a forceful stream of water, and perhaps light scrubbing with soap, will help prevent infection.

3. Protect the wound with sterile gauze or a bandage strip. If the player continues to participate in activity, apply protective padding over the injured area.

4. Remove and dispose of gloves carefully to prevent yourself and others from coming into contact with blood.

Coaching Tip
Don't let a fear of acquired immune deficiency syndrome (AIDS) or other communicable diseases stop you from helping a player. You are at risk only if you allow contaminated blood to come in contact with an open wound on your body, so the examination gloves that you wear will protect you from AIDS should one of your players carry this disease. Check with your sport director, your league, or the local hospital for more information about protecting yourself and your players from AIDS.

For bloody noses not associated with serious facial injury, have the player sit and lean slightly forward. Then pinch his or her nostrils shut. If the bleeding continues for several minutes, or if the player has a history of nosebleeds, seek medical assistance.

Strains and Sprains   The physical demands of cricket training and games often result in injury to the muscles or tendons (strains) or to the ligaments (sprains). When your players suffer minor strains or sprains, immediately apply the PRICE method of injury care:

P   Protect the player and injured body part from further danger or trauma.

R   Rest the area to avoid further damage and foster healing.

I   Ice the area to reduce swelling and pain.

C   Compress the area by securing an ice bag in place with an elastic wrap.

E   Elevate the injury above heart level to keep the blood from pooling in the area.

Bumps and Bruises Inevitably, cricket players make contact with each other, with the ball, and with the ground. If the force applied to a body part at impact is great enough, a bump or bruise will result. Many players continue playing with such sore spots, but if the bump or bruise is large and painful, you should act appropriately. Again, use the PRICE method for injury care, and monitor the injury. If swelling, discolouration, and pain have lessened, the player may resume participation with protective padding; if not, the player should be examined by a medical professional.

Serious Injuries

Head, neck, and back injuries; fractures; and injuries that cause a player to lose consciousness are among a class of injuries that you cannot and should not try to treat yourself. In these cases follow the emergency plan outlined on page 43. We do want to examine more closely, however, your role in preventing heat cramps, heat exhaustion, and heatstroke.

Heat Cramps Tough practices combined with heat stress and substantial fluid loss from sweating can provoke muscle cramps, commonly known as heat cramps. Cramping is most common when the weather is hot. Depending on your location, it might be hot early in the season, which can be problematic because players are likely less conditioned and less adapted to heat, or later in the season, when players are better conditioned but still not used to playing in high temperatures. A cramp—a severe tightening of the muscle—can drop players and prevent continued play. Dehydration, electrolyte loss, and fatigue are contributing factors. The immediate treatment is to have players cool off and slowly stretch the contracted muscle. Players may return to play later that same day or the next day provided the cramp doesn't cause a muscle strain.

Heat Exhaustion Heat exhaustion is a shock-like condition caused by dehydration and electrolyte depletion. Symptoms include headache, nausea, dizziness, chills, fatigue, and extreme thirst. Profuse sweating is a key sign of heat exhaustion. Other signs include pale, cool, and clammy skin; rapid, weak pulse; loss of coordination; and dilated pupils.

A player suffering from heat exhaustion should rest in a cool, shaded area; drink cool fluids, particularly those containing electrolytes; and apply ice to the neck, back, or abdomen to help cool the body. If you believe a player is suffering from heat exhaustion, seek medical attention. Under no condition should the player return to activity that day or before she regains all the weight lost through sweat. If the player must see a physician, she shouldn't return to the team until receiving a written release from the physician.

Heatstroke Heatstroke is a life-threatening condition in which the body stops sweating and body temperature rises dangerously high. Heatstroke occurs when dehydration causes a malfunction in the body's temperature control centre in the brain. Symptoms include nausea, confusion, irritability, fatigue, and the feeling of being extremely hot. Signs include hot, dry, and flushed or red skin (this is a key sign); lack of sweat; rapid pulse; rapid breathing; constricted pupils; vomiting; diahorrea; and possibly seizures, unconsciousness, or respiratory or cardiac arrest.

If you suspect a player is suffering from heatstroke, send for emergency medical assistance immediately, and cool the player as quickly as possible. Remove excess clothing and equipment, and cool the player's body with cool, wet towels, by pouring cool water over him or by placing the player in a cold bath. Apply ice packs to the armpits, neck, back, and abdomen and between the legs. If the player is conscious, give him cool fluids to drink. If the player is unconscious or falls unconscious, place him on his side to allow fluids and vomit to drain from the mouth. A player who has suffered heatstroke may not return to the team until receiving a written release from a physician.

Protecting Yourself

When one of your players is injured, naturally your first concern is the player's well-being. After all, your desire to help youngsters is what made you want to coach. Unfortunately, you must consider something else as well: Can you be held liable for the injury?

From a legal standpoint, a coach must fulfil nine duties. The following is a summary of your legal duties:

1. Provide a safe environment.
2. Properly plan the activity.
3. Provide adequate and proper equipment.
4. Match players appropriately.
5. Warn of inherent risks in the sport.
6. Supervise the activity closely.
7. Evaluate players for injury or incapacitation.
8. Know emergency procedures, CPR, and first aid (ECB coaches requirement).
9. Keep adequate records.

In addition to fulfilling these nine legal duties, you should check your organisation's insurance coverage and your own personal insurance coverage to make sure these policies will properly protect you from liability.

Player's safety is important; be prepared to do everything you can to eliminate accidents where possible. By its very nature though, cricket played with a hard ball carries the possibility to cause injuries. You may not be able to avoid incidents of strains, sprains, breaks, and pulled muscles, but you can be prepared to treat them by having items on hand to do so.

5

Making Practices Fun and Practical

In the past cricket has placed too much emphasis on learning skills and not enough on learning how to play skilfully (that is, how to use those skills in competition). The games approach, in contrast to the traditional approach, emphasises learning what to do first, and then how to do it. Moreover, the games approach lets kids discover what to do in the game not by your telling them but by their experiencing it. This approach is a guided discovery method of teaching that empowers your kids to solve the problems that arise in games, which is a large part of the fun in learning.

On the surface it would seem to make sense to introduce cricket using the traditional approach—by first teaching the basic skills of the sport and then the tactics of the game—but disadvantages have been discovered in doing so. First, the traditional approach teaches the skills of the sport out of the context of the game. Kids might learn to catch, throw, and hit the ball, but they find it difficult to use these skills in the real game because they don't yet understand the basic tactical skills of cricket and don't appreciate how best to use their newfound technical skills in actual competition. Second, learning skills by doing drills outside of the context of the game is downright boring. The single biggest turnoff in sports is overorganised instruction that deprives kids of their intrinsic desire to play the game.

The games approach is taught using a four-step process:

1. Play a modified game.
2. Help players understand the game (i.e., discover what they need to do to play the game successfully).
3. Teach the skills of the game.
4. Practice the skills in another game.

Step 1: Play a Modified Game

It's the first day of practice; some of your young players are eager to get started, while others are obviously apprehensive. Some have rarely hit a ball, most don't know the rules, and few know the positions in cricket. What do you do?

If you used the traditional approach, you would start with a quick warm-up activity, then line the players up for a simple drill and go from there. In the games approach, you begin by playing a modified game that is developmentally appropriate for the level of the players and designed to focus on learning a specific part of the game.

Modifying the game lets you emphasise a limited number of situations in the game. This is one way to guide your players to discover certain game tactics. For instance, you set up the fielders and have a batsman facing a nonstriker. The goal of the game for the fielders is to make a run out. Playing the game this way forces players to think about what they need to do to make that run out.

Activities Checklist

When developing activities for your youth cricket programme, here are a few questions to ask yourself:

- Are the activities fun?
- Are the activities organised?
- Are the players involved in the activities?
- Are creativity and decision making evident?
- Are the spaces used appropriate?
- Is your feedback appropriate?
- Are there implications for the game?

Step 2: Help Players Understand the Game

As your players are playing a game, look for the right spot to "freeze" the action, step in, and ask questions about errors that you're seeing. When you do this, you help them better understand the objective of the game, how to achieve the objective, and what skills to use.

Asking the right questions is an important part of teaching. Essentially you'll be asking your players, "What do you need to do to succeed in this situation?" Sometimes players simply need more time playing the game, or you might need to modify the game further so that it's even easier for them to discover what they need to do. It might take more patience on your part, but it's a powerful way to learn. For example, assume your players are playing a game in which the objective is to make a run out, but they are having trouble doing so. Interrupt the action and ask the following questions:

- What are you supposed to do in this game?
- What do you have to do to make sure you collect the ball correctly?
- Who backs up the stumps if the ball is hit to the off side?
- Who backs up the stumps if the ball is hit to the leg side?

> **Coaching Tip**
>
> If your players have trouble understanding what to do, phrase your questions to let them choose between two options. For example, if you ask, "What's the best way to get the ball to the stumps when you're very close to them?" and they reply, "Throw it," then ask, "Throw it underarm or overarm?"

At first, asking the right questions might seem difficult because your players have little or no experience with the game. If you've learned sport through the traditional approach, you'll be tempted to tell your players how to play the game rather than waste time asking questions. In the games approach, however, resist this powerful temptation to tell your players what to do.

Instead, through modified games and skilful questioning on your part, your players should come to realise on their own that tactical awareness and accurate fielding skills are essential to their success in keeping batsmen from stealing singles. Just as important, as you can see, instead of telling them what the critical skills are, you led them to this discovery, which is a crucial part of the games approach.

Step 3: Teach the Skills of the Game

Only when your players recognise the skills they need to be successful in the game do you want to teach these skills through activities focused on game situations. This is when you use a more traditional approach to teaching sports skills, the IDEA approach, which we'll discuss in chapter 6. This type of teaching breaks down the skills of the game and should be implemented early in the season to make games more fun and so players can begin attaining skills.

Step 4: Practice the Skills in Another Game

You want your players to experience success as they're learning skills, and the best way to experience this success early on is to create an advantage for the players. Once they have practiced the skill, as outlined in step 3, you can then put them in another game situation—this time with a fielding advantage (e.g., instead of having just a few fielders, add an additional fielder between both sets of stumps on the leg side and off side). The prevailing notion is that this setup (more fielders) makes it more likely that your players can stop the ball and make the run out.

Coaching Tip

Some cricket skills don't easily lend themselves to providing an advantage. For example, the basic mechanics of throwing the ball, swinging a bat, or making a catch are best taught with individual attention to each player, often as players practice with a partner. Tactics, as well as team plays, however, are ideal for game-like settings.

It's usually best to first use a normal situation (i.e., typical number of fielders) and then introduce games in which one side has an advantage. The reasoning behind this is to introduce players to a situation similar to what they'll experience in competition and to let them discover the challenges they face in performing the necessary skill. Then you teach them the skill, have them practice it, and put them back in another game, this time using an advantage to give them a greater chance of success.

As players improve their skills, you might do away with the advantage. Having extra fielders will eventually make things too easy and won't challenge your players to hone their skills. When this time comes, lessen the advantage, or decide that they're ready to practice the skill in regular competition. The key is to set up situations in which your players experience success but remain challenged in doing so. This takes careful monitoring on your part, but having kids play altered games as they are learning skills is an effective way to help them learn and improve.

And that's the games approach. Your players get to play more in practice, and once they learn how skills fit into their performance and enjoyment of the game, they'll be more motivated to work on those skills, which helps them to succeed.

6

Teaching and Shaping Skills

Coaching cricket involves teaching kids how to play the game by teaching them skills, fitness, and values. It also involves coaching players before, during, and after contests. Teaching and coaching are closely related, but there are important differences. In this chapter we focus on principles of teaching, especially on teaching technical and tactical skills, though these principles apply to teaching fitness concepts and values as well. Armed with these principles, you'll be able to design effective and efficient practices and understand how to deal with misbehaviour. Then you'll be able to teach the skills and plays outlined in the chapters ahead that are necessary to be successful in cricket.

Teaching Cricket Skills

The skill of any great coach is to make teaching simple. That means keeping things clear and easy to understand. One of the challenges of coaching is taking relatively complex information for young players to understand and delivering it so it comes across as logical and sequential. If you put yourself in the position of the players you coach and ask yourself, "What do I need to know next?" you help yourself become a more logical coach.

Teaching is not only, or even mainly, about qualifications. Many people believe that the only qualification needed to teach a skill is to have performed it. Although it's helpful to have performed the skill, teaching it successfully requires much more than that. And even if you haven't performed the skill yourself, you can still learn to teach the skill, keeping in mind the useful acronym IDEA:

I	Introduce the skill.
D	Demonstrate the skill.
E	Explain the skill.
A	Attend to players practicing the skill.

Introduce the Skill

Players, especially those who are young and inexperienced, need to know what skill they are learning and why they are learning it. Use the following three steps every time you introduce a skill to your players:

1. Get your players' attention.
2. Name the skill.
3. Explain the importance of the skill.

> **Coaching Tip**
> Writing out in detail each skill you will teach clarifies what you will say and how you will demonstrate and teach the skills to your players.

Get Your Players' Attention

Because youngsters are easily distracted, you need to get their attention somehow. Some coaches relate news items or stories. Others tell jokes. Still others simply project enthusiasm to get their players to listen. Whatever method you use, speak slightly above your normal volume, and look your players in the eye when you speak.

Position players so they can see and hear you. Arrange them in two or three evenly spaced rows facing you. Make sure they aren't looking into the sun or at a distracting activity. Ask them if they can see you before you begin to speak.

Name the Skill

If there's more than one name for the skill you're introducing, decide as a staff before the start of the season which one you'll use and stick with it. This prevents confusion and allows for clear communication among players. When you introduce the new skill, call it by name several times so your players automatically correlate the name with the skill in later discussions.

Explain the Importance of the Skill

One of the most difficult lessons to learn in coaching is this: You must learn to let players learn. Sport skills should be taught so they have meaning to the child, not just meaning to the coach. Although the importance of a skill might be apparent to you, your players might be less able to see how the skill will help them become better cricket players. Give them a reason for learning the skill, and describe how the skill relates to more advanced skills.

Demonstrate the Skill

The demonstration step is the most important part of teaching a sports skill to players who have never done anything closely resembling it. They need a picture, not just words, so they can see how the skill is performed. If you are unable to execute the skill correctly, ask an assistant coach, one of your players, or someone else to perform the demonstration.

These tips help make demonstrations more effective:

- Use correct form (we have mentioned this in a previous chapter, and it is vital).
- Demonstrate the skill several times (some players might have missed something).
- Slow the action, if possible, during one or two performances so players can see every movement involved in the skill (doing this also shows them how to tap into their muscle memory).
- Perform the skill at different angles so your players can get a full perspective.
- Demonstrate the skill with both sides of the body (if this is not possible, tell opposite-hand players that you are their mirror).

Explain the Skill

Players learn more effectively when given a brief explanation of the skill along with the demonstration. Use simple terms and, if possible, relate the skill to previously learned skills. Ask players if they understand your description. A good technique is to ask them to repeat your explanation. Ask questions such as, "What are you going to do first?" and "Then what?" If players look confused or uncertain, repeat your explanation and demonstration. If possible, use different words so your players get a chance to understand the skill from a different perspective.

Complex skills are often better understood when they are explained in more manageable parts. For instance, if you want to teach your players how to field a ball, you might take the following steps:

1. Show them a correct performance of the entire skill, and explain the skill's function in cricket.
2. Break the skill down and point out its component parts to your players.
3. Have players perform each of the component skills you have taught them, such as assuming the ready position and moving to the ball.
4. After players have demonstrated their ability to perform the separate parts of the skill in sequence, re-explain the entire skill.
5. Have players practice the skill in game-like conditions.

Young players have short attention spans, so a long demonstration or explanation of a skill might be lost on them. Spend no more than a few minutes altogether on the introduction, demonstration, and explanation phases. Then involve the players in drills or games so they can perform the skill.

How to Run Your Drills

Before running a drill that teaches technique, do the following:

- Name the drill.
- Explain the skill or skills to be taught.
- Position players correctly.
- Explain what the drill will accomplish.
- State the command that will start the drill.
- State the command that will end the drill, such as a whistle.

After introducing the drill and repeating it a few times, you'll find that merely calling out the name of the drill is sufficient, and your players will automatically line up in the proper position to run the drill and practice the skill.

Attend to Players Practicing the Skill

If the skill you selected was within your players' capabilities and you have done an effective job of introducing, demonstrating, and explaining it, your players should be ready to attempt the skill. Some players, especially younger players, might need to be physically guided through the movements during their first few attempts. Walking unsure players through the skill helps them gain confidence to execute the skill on their own.

Your teaching duties don't end when all your players have demonstrated that they understand how to perform a skill. In fact, as you help your players improve their skills your teaching role is just beginning. A significant part of teaching consists of closely observing the hit-and-miss trial performances of your players. You will shape players' skills by detecting errors and correcting them, using positive feedback. Keep in mind that your positive feedback has a great influence on your players' motivation to practice and improve.

Some players might require individual instruction, so set aside a time before, during, or after practice to give individual help.

Coaching Tip

Technology improvements have created an opportunity to bring new demonstration methods to the practice field. Many cricket skill DVDs are on the market, so consider using these as tools to show skills, especially if you have difficulty demonstrating a skill. This method is particularly effective with older players, who are better able to transfer skills they see on the screen to their own performance.

Learning Preferences

When shaping your players' skills, it's very helpful to understand their individual learning preferences. Our learning preferences are how we as individuals most easily learn new things. For our purposes in teaching cricket, we'll say that every player has a combination of three styles of learning: auditory, visual, and kinaesthetic. (Reading and writing is a fourth style, but for net coaching and skills acquisition we'll focus on just the three.)

An auditory approach to teaching is likely the least effective for most players. If you only stand there talking to players, telling them what to do, barking instructions, or shouting from the end of a net while hiding behind a bowling machine, don't be surprised if your players struggle to improve. If you have ever experienced a lecture or presentation in which someone drones on and on about something, you'll understand why it's very hard to learn much, let alone remember much, about what you've heard. Rabbiting on about this and that only puts your audience to sleep. That's why an auditory style is usually ineffective in isolation. A dependence on *telling* people things typically doesn't work.

A visual approach to teaching is all about showing players how to execute. Demonstrations, video clips, pictures, and television are all useful methods of showing. Most kids who watch cricket on television will at some stage try out for themselves the skills they have seen. Part of this is that children tend to be great mimics. With this in mind, ensure that when you do demonstrations yourself they are *really* good—because your players will be copying what you do. A poor demonstration not only depletes your credibility (because some players will recognise how poorly you are doing the skill) but also promotes poor execution (because other players will try to copy your poor execution).

On the other hand, a good demonstration can be uplifting, inspirational, and have a *wow* effect on your players. For some coaches working with players on hard-hit shots, the sheer power of their demonstration had their kids talking long afterward. In other such cases, a clear visual demonstration of power—such as violently uprooting stumps while demonstrating fast bowling, turning a ball square during a leg break demo, or billowing out some distant net with a strong throw during a ground fielding exercise—affects young cricketers far more than mere words can. Of course you might not be able to execute such demonstrations yourself (though if you can, go ahead!), but you'll find that skilled, experienced players are often willing to help out. If no such players are available, do the best you can, as long as the execution is correct. You might not wow your players, but they'll get the point and understand how to execute.

Far and away the fastest way most people learn a sporting skill is kinaesthetically—that is, when we execute a skill ourselves. This kind of learning is all about involvement, interaction, feeling, and emotion and can impact quite dramatically on skill acquisition. That's because to change muscle memory (the body's ability to do a task automatically without you thinking about it) you have to tap into this part.

Questioning

Sometimes as a coach you simply must teach technique to a group of people when no one in the group knows how to execute the particular skill. In such cases there is still room for you to make your players feel they are leading much of the session (and thus be more interested in what you're teaching). The secret is in questioning them. By using effective questioning you can draw out what they know and then guide them toward the answer.

To begin, you should have an idea of what you want to achieve from a session. What is your intended outcome? You must always have an intention for a particular lesson, or at least an idea of one, before you try to communicate the lesson to your players. If you don't, you are likely conducting a pointless practice.

Although *you* know where you want to take a session, you might want to ask your players for their input to make them feel they are guiding the session, and thus an important part, which keeps them alert and interested. Even with young players you can use effective questioning to create an inclusive atmosphere within the boundaries you set for the session. Questioning allows players to show what they know and encourages them to speak up. Keep in mind, though, that young players will tend to tell you what they think you want to hear. That's why whenever you get an answer to a question you should try to drill a bit deeper. Try asking five questions. Because if you ask a player five questions, each time using his or her previous answer as the basis for your next question, you will often find the *real* reason for his or her initial response. By delving deeper you sometimes discover the truth. Here's an example:

A coach was working with a young player who, when asked what was wrong with a shot that went in the air in the nets (*first question*), answered, "I didn't get to the pitch of the ball." This answer was what he thought the coach wanted to hear. The coach then asked, "Why didn't you get to the pitch of it?" (*second question*). The player answered, "I didn't stride far enough." The coach further probed, "Did something stop you from striding far enough?" (*third question*), to which the player replied, "My weight was on my back foot." The coach said, "Okay, good. So what made you go onto your back foot with your weight?" (*fourth question*). The player thought about it and answered, "I have always done that." The coach then asked the million-dollar question: "Always? Can you tell me why you always do that?" (*fifth question*). The player looked at the coach and said, "I once got hit by a ball on a bad pitch."

The first answer the player gave to the question was accurate, but it didn't get at the underlying problem as to why he hit the ball in the air. By finding that out, the coach then worked on the player's confidence to get forward and play the shot correctly—which he knew how to play, by the way. This player's issue was mental, not technical. This is an example of truly outstanding coaching because the problem was determined and solved. If you don't find the true root of a problem, you can't solve the problem.

Many of the best coaches get their students to walk through their bowling action with their eyes closed so they really *feel* what's going on in their action. If we want to communicate change, we have to do this with the mind's approval. So using balance and awareness is a large part of helping create an understanding of what that player does.

To put all this together, if we tell a player what to do (auditory), then show them what to do with an effective demonstration (visual), and then get them to execute the skill themselves (kinaesthetic), we can finally communicate feedback to them and help them acquire the skill. If you really want to nail down the learning process, you can introduce the fourth style, which this book promised to get to. This style is reading and writing and involves the player writing down what they have done during session. This last step completes the learning loop and is a vital way to ensure you have communicated correctly.

> **Coaching Tip**
>
> Help young players to learn by tapping into their emotions, such as feeling. One of the most effective forms of questioning requires your students to give you feedback. Questions such as, "How did that feel?" and "What did you notice about your balance when you did that?" supply you with instant feedback. Open questioning of this kind (avoiding simple yes or no answers) and individual targeting helps both you and the player better understand what is being learned.

Helping Players Improve Skills

Once you have taught your players the fundamentals of a skill, your focus is on helping them to improve it. Players learn skills and improve on them at different rates, so don't get frustrated if progress seems slow. Help them improve by shaping their skills and detecting and correcting errors.

Shaping Players' Skills

One of your principal teaching duties is to reward positive effort and behaviour, in terms of successful skill execution, when you see it. When a player makes a good shot in practice, you immediately say, "That's the way to keep your head over the ball! Good shot!" or something to that effect. This verbal feedback, plus a smile and a thumbs-up gesture, goes a long way toward reinforcing proper technique. However, long, dry spells can sometimes occur before you see correct techniques to reinforce. It's difficult to reward players when they don't execute skills correctly. How can you shape their skills if this is the case?

Shaping skills takes practice on your players' part and patience on yours. Expect your players to make errors. Telling the player who made the good hit that she did a good job doesn't ensure that she'll have the same success next time. Seeing inconsistency in your players' technique can be frustrating. It's even more challenging to stay positive when your players repeatedly perform a skill incorrectly or show a lack of enthusiasm for learning. It can certainly be frustrating to see players who seemingly don't heed your advice continue to make the same mistakes.

Remember that it's normal to get frustrated when teaching skills. But part of successful coaching is controlling your frustration. Instead of getting upset, try these six guidelines for shaping skills:

1. *Think small initially.*

   Reward the first signs of behaviour that approximate what you want. Then reward closer and closer approximations of the desired behaviour. In short, use your reward power to shape the behaviour you seek.

2. *Break skills into small steps.*

   For instance, in learning to field the ball and throw to the stumps, one of your players does well in getting into position and watching the ball into his hand, but she performs a flat-footed throw to the stumps. Reinforce the correct techniques of getting into proper position and watching the ball into the hands, and teach her how to set up and prepare to throw. Once she masters this, focus on getting her to complete the skill by pushing off the back leg after moving forward and throwing the ball over the top.

3. *Develop one component of a skill at a time.*

   Don't try to shape two components of a skill at once. For example, in batting, players must begin with a proper grip, get in a comfortable and appropriate stance, and use proper mechanics in the stride and downswing. Players should focus first on one aspect (grip), then on another (stance), and then another (stride and downswing). Players who have problems mastering a skill are often trying to improve two or more components at once. Help these players isolate a single component.

4. *Use reinforcement only occasionally, for the best examples.*

   By focusing only on the best examples you'll help players continue to improve once they have mastered the basics. Using occasional reinforcement during practice allows players more contact time with the bat or ball instead of constantly stopping to listen to instructions. Cricket skills are best learned through repetition, such as drills and game-like activities; giving players time with the bat and ball makes the best use of practice.

5. *Relax your reward standards.*

   As a new skill is learned, or as two or more skills are combined into one action, a temporary decline in performance might occur, and you might need to relax your expectations. For example, a bowler has learned how to bowl an outswinger with a basic bowling action and wrist position but is now learning how to modify that technique to develop a new delivery. While the player is learning to adjust the grip and getting the timing right or wrist position altered, both deliveries might be poor.

A similar degeneration of skills can occur during growth spurts while the coordination of muscles, tendons, and ligaments catches up to the growth of bones.

6. *Go back to the basics.*

   If a well-learned skill gets worse over a period of time, you might need to restore the skill by going back to the basics. If necessary, practice the skill using an activity in which the players have less pressure from opponents so they can relearn the skill (for example, let bowlers practice with only a set of stumps, not adding a batter until they're comfortable with the new delivery).

Detecting and Correcting Errors

Good coaches recognise that players make two types of errors: learning errors and performance errors. Learning errors occur because players don't know how to perform a skill; that is, they have not yet developed the correct motor pattern in the brain (muscle memory) to perform a particular skill. Performance errors are made not because players don't know how to execute the skill but because they have made a mistake in executing what they do know. There is no easy way to know whether a player is committing a learning or a performance error; part of the art of coaching is learning to sort out which type of error each mistake is.

The process of helping your players correct errors begins with observing and evaluating performances to determine if the mistakes are learning or performance errors. Watch carefully to see if a player routinely makes the errors in both practice and game settings, or if the errors tend to occur in game settings only. If the latter is the case, then the player is committing a performance error. For performance errors, you need to look for the reason a player is not performing as well as he can; perhaps he's nervous, or maybe he gets distracted by the game setting. If the mistake is a learning error, you need to help him learn the skill, which is the focus of this section.

When correcting learning errors, there is no substitute for your own mastery of the skill. The better you understand a skill—not only how it is executed but also what causes learning errors—the more helpful you will be in correcting mistakes.

One of the most common coaching mistakes is providing inaccurate feedback and advice on how to correct errors. Don't rush into error correction; wrong feedback or poor advice hinders the learning process more than no feedback or advice at all. If you're uncertain about the cause

Coaching Tip
For older age groups or players with advanced skill, coaches can ask players to self-coach. With proper guidance and a positive team environment, young players can consider how they execute a skill and how they might be able to do it better. Self-coaching is best done at practice, when players can experiment with learning new skills.

of the problem or how to correct it, continue to observe and analyse until you are more certain. As a rule, you should see the error repeated several times before attempting to correct it.

Correct One Error at a Time

Suppose one of your boundary fielders is having trouble with fielding. The player tends to charge in on the ball and often must reverse direction when the ball goes over her head. And for balls that she is in position to catch, she uses only one hand. What do you do?

First, decide which error to correct first; as mentioned, players learn best when correcting one error at a time. Determine whether one error is causing the other; if so, have the player correct that error first because it might eliminate the other error. In this case, however, neither error is causing the other. In such cases, players should correct the error that is easiest to correct and will bring the greatest improvement when remedied. For this player, the error that is easiest to correct is probably getting back quickly on balls hit over her head. If balls are repeatedly going over her head, she needs to position deeper. If balls go over her head only occasionally, she needs to break her instinct of running at the ball on every ball that goes up. Once she improves her ability to judge high catches and get in proper position, then you can work on her catching the ball with two hands. Note that improvement in the first area might even motivate her to correct the other error.

Use Positive Feedback to Correct Errors

The positive approach to correcting errors includes emphasising what to do instead of what not to do. Use praise, rewards, and encouragement to correct errors. Acknowledge correct performance as well as efforts to improve. By using positive feedback, you can help your players feel good about themselves and promote a strong desire to achieve.

When working with one player at a time, the positive approach to correcting errors has four steps:

1. *Praise effort and correct performance.*

   Praise players for trying to perform a skill correctly and for performing any parts of it correctly. Praise players immediately after they perform the skill, if possible. Keep the praise simple: "Good try," "Well done," "Good form," or "That's the way to follow through." You can also use nonverbal feedback, such as smiling, clapping your hands, or any facial or body expression that shows approval.

   Be sincere with your praise. Don't indicate that a player's effort was good when it wasn't. Usually players know when they have made a sincere effort to execute a skill correctly, and they'll perceive undeserved praise for what it is—untruthful feedback to make them feel good. Likewise, don't indicate that a player's performance was correct when it wasn't.

2. *Give simple and precise feedback to correct errors.*

Don't burden a player with a long or detailed explanation of how to correct an error. Give just enough feedback that the player can correct one error at a time. Before giving feedback, recognise that some players readily accept it immediately after the error; others respond better if you slightly delay the correction.

For errors that are complicated to explain and difficult to correct, try the following:

- Explain and demonstrate what the player should have done. Do not demonstrate what the player did wrong.
- Explain the cause (or causes) of the error if it isn't obvious.
- Explain why you are recommending the correction you have selected, if it's not obvious.

3. *Make sure players understand your feedback.*

If players don't understand your feedback, they won't be able to correct their errors. Ask them to repeat the feedback and explain and demonstrate how to use it. If they can't do this, be patient and present your feedback again. Then have them repeat the feedback after you're finished.

4. *Provide an environment that motivates players to improve.*

Your players won't always be able to correct their errors immediately even when they understand your feedback. Encourage them to "see it through and work with it" when they seem discouraged or when corrections are difficult. For more difficult corrections, remind them that it takes time to improve, and that improvement will happen only if they work at it. Encourage players with little self-confidence. Say something like, "You were hitting much better today; with practice, you'll be able to keep your head still and make consistent contact."

Other players might be very self-motivated and need little help from you in this area; with these players you can practically ignore step 4 when correcting an error. Although motivation comes from within, try to provide an environment of positive instruction and encouragement to help your players improve.

A final note on correcting errors: Team sports such as cricket provide unique challenges in this endeavour. How do you provide individual feedback in a group setting using a positive approach? Instead of yelling across the field during practice to correct an error (and embarrassing the player), substitute for the player who erred. Then make the correction in the pavilion, nets, changing room, or to the side of the playing field. This type of feedback has several advantages:

- The player will be more receptive to the one-on-one feedback.
- The other players are still active and practicing skills, unable to hear your discussion.

- Because the rest of the team is still playing, you'll feel compelled to make your comments simple and concise, which is more helpful to the player.

This doesn't mean you can't use the team setting to give specific positive feedback. You can do so to emphasise correct group and individual performances. Use this team feedback approach only for positive statements, though. Save negative feedback for individual discussion.

Dealing With Misbehaviour

Young players misbehave at times—it's only natural. There are two ways to respond to misbehaviour: through extinction or discipline.

Extinction

Ignoring a misbehaviour—neither rewarding nor disciplining it—is called extinction. This can be effective under certain circumstances. In some situations, disciplining young people's misbehaviour only encourages them to act up further because of the attention they get. Ignoring misbehaviour teaches youngsters that such behaviour is not worth your attention.

Sometimes, though, you can't wait for a behaviour to fizzle out. When players cause danger to themselves or others or disrupt the activities of others, you need to take immediate action. Tell the offending player that the behaviour must stop and that discipline will follow if it doesn't. If the player doesn't stop misbehaving after the warning, use discipline.

Extinction also doesn't work well when a misbehaviour is self-rewarding. For example, you might be able to keep from grimacing if a youngster kicks you in the shin, but even so, he still knows you were hurt. Therein lies the reward. In these circumstances, it's necessary to discipline the player for the undesirable behaviour.

Extinction works best in situations in which players are seeking recognition through mischievous behaviours, clowning, or grandstanding. Usually, if you are patient, their failure to get your attention makes the behaviour disappear. However, be alert that you don't extinguish desirable behaviour. When youngsters do something well, they expect to be positively reinforced. Not rewarding them will likely make them discontinue the desired behaviour.

Discipline

Some educators say we should never discipline young people but should only reinforce their positive behaviours. They argue that discipline does not work, creates hostility, and sometimes develops avoidance behaviours that might be less desirable than the original problem behaviour. It is true that discipline does not always work and that it can create problems when used ineffectively, but when used appropriately, discipline is effective in eliminating undesirable behaviours without creating undesirable consequences. You must use discipline effectively because it's sometimes impossible to guide players through positive reinforcement and extinction alone. Discipline is part of a positive approach when these guidelines are followed:

> **Coaching Tip**
>
> Involve older players in the process of setting team rules and the consequences for breaking them. Players 12 years and older are capable of brainstorming ideas for discipline in common situations, such as being late for practice, criticising another player, or talking back to the coach. Once you've agreed on a list of rules and consequences, have each player sign the rules to cement their willingness to abide by them.

- Discipline in a corrective way to help players improve now and in the future. Don't discipline to retaliate and make yourself feel better.

- Impose discipline in an impersonal way when players break team rules or otherwise misbehave. Shouting at or scolding players indicates that your attitude is vengeful.

- Once a good rule has been agreed on, ensure that players who violate it experience the unpleasant consequences of their misbehaviour. Don't wave discipline threateningly over their heads. Just do it, but warn a player once before disciplining.

- Be consistent in administering discipline.

- Take care not to use discipline to inadvertently punish a young player trying to be creative.

- Don't discipline using consequences that might cause you guilt. If you can't think of an appropriate consequence right away, tell the player you will talk with him or her after you think about it. Consider involving the player in coming up with a consequence.

- Once the discipline is completed, don't make players feel as though they're in the doghouse. Always make them feel they're valued members of the team.

- Make sure that what you think is discipline isn't perceived by the player as a positive reinforcement; for instance, keeping a player out of doing a certain activity or portion of the training session might be just what the player desired.

- Never discipline players for making errors when they are playing.

- Never use physical activity—running laps or doing push-ups—as discipline. Doing so only makes players resent physical activity, which we want them to learn to enjoy throughout their lives.

- Discipline sparingly. Constant discipline and criticism make players resent you and turn their interests elsewhere.

As with any good coaching, you should always think about how you would wish to be coached and then try to apply that to situations. Naturally, there's a fine line between being bossy and being the boss, so be aware how you are coming across in the minds of those you work with. Most young cricketers crave fairness and encouragement.

Some coaches show their disappointment in a result, situation, or outcome by using "naughty nets," in which extra training sessions are implemented on kids. Think long and hard about using practice as a negative reinforcement. Sometimes when things go wrong it's best to not use this type of practice as discipline but rather to let players reflect themselves. The message is: Be smart. Remember that players themselves are usually the most disappointed when things go wrong.

7

Coaching Fielding

An inescapable fact of cricket is that everyone on the team has to field. What has happened over the last few years is that fielding has become far more important in team selection and to the outcome of matches. The art of fielding, or at least the application of the skills of fielding, is now a crucial part of the game. Coaches today often base their game-day decisions on which player fields better than another or if a certain player is a liability on the field. That's why it's vital that everyone on a squad spends time practicing fielding skills. Half a match is spent in the field, so why not perfect what you need to be good?

Many players find fielding boring. Players who only bat sometimes don't realise that they can save 20 to 30 runs in the field. These are 20 to 30 runs their team doesn't have to score. It's vital you for you as a coach to instil a run-saving mentality into your players from the start. This means they can enjoy what they do and feel they are making a critical contribution to the team's cause.

Fielding becomes even more important if a player has had a bad day and failed with the bat. The player can still make a match-winning contribution with a brilliant catch or run out or by diving to make a run-saving play in the field. The days of "carrying" someone on the field or having a "passenger" have long gone. It's imperative in modern cricket that all players can field well.

A key to getting your players excited about fielding is to make skill drills fun and competitive. You'll get the very best from a team when everyone feels a part of the squad and when all players pull together to achieve a result. This requires pride in performance. As coach, your role is to encourage your players to do their very best at all times. You don't want sloppy practices. You want to see your players keep up their energy levels and maintain good technique. When drilling, remember that practice doesn't make perfect—it makes *permanent*. Only perfect practice makes perfect. Set out your drills clearly, demonstrate them well, and ensure that all players can understand what you want the outcome to be. If you do all this, you have a great chance of creating a squad of players who are exceptional in the field. Above all, when you do skill sessions, make them *fun*. Even the simplest of sessions to make a basic point can be enjoyable if it's filled with action and enthusiasm.

If you can teach correct technique for a skill, groove it, reinforce it, and help your players have success with it, the skill will become an automatic reflex (via muscle memory) and a learned experience. Muscle memory is the body's ability to repeat a movement over and over without a conscious thought process. All sport involves players gaining muscle memory. The youngest of players will have none to speak of as they are learning things from scratch. Older players have muscle memory from previous matches, practices, seasons, and experiences. This is where the saying "you can't teach an old dog new tricks" comes from. However, like many sayings, this one is inaccurate because anyone can learn a new skill. But it does take longer to teach a skill if you have to change a player's muscle memory—which is why it's important to get to your cricket players early and help them establish good habits.

Coaching Fielding Basics

Certain fielding fundamentals need to be coached. These include stopping the ball, catching the ball, and throwing the ball. The better your fielders execute these basics, the better they'll become as team members, and their value to the side will be greatly enhanced.

Stopping the Ball

Stopping the ball is getting your body or hands behind the ball to effect a good piece of ground fielding. Regardless of whether a fielder is attacking the ball or merely trying to stop it, the key to ground fielding is that the player's body is kept low as he prepares to collect the ball. It's preferable to be in a position of alertness, with slightly bent knees, weight moving toward the ball, and body angled forward in a semicrouching position. This helps keep eyes firmly on any uneven bounce the ball makes. The eyes should watch the ball all the way into the hands.

In addition, a fielder must ensure that any return to the wicket keeper is on the full, which goes straight to the target without batting. This is the fastest delivery of the ball and the easiest for the wicket keeper to catch. Also, fielders should communicate with all players around them to ensure they are taking the right option. It might be that throwing the ball to the bowling end is a better thing to do; if so, other players can help by calling out where the ball should go.

When it comes to infielders and outfielders, you must instil the importance of "walking in" as the bowler runs in to bowl. This helps with anticipation and ensures that their feet are moving and not planted or static. You don't want fielders caught on their heels or, worse, losing focus and suddenly having to react to something when they're not ready. So just as the batsman is about to hit the ball, the fielders will take short steps toward the batter and be ready to move in the direction the ball is hit. The movements of fielders should be light, which means staying on the balls of the feet. Imagine a football goalkeeper ready to move left or right, or prepared to dive up or down. This is how the fielder in cricket should look. Knees are flexed at the point the ball is hit; head and eyes are fixed on the ball, as shown in figure 7.1. The fielder can then decide which way to move—and fast.

Also, by watching the "shape" of the shot the batsman plays and his or her footwork, arm movements, and position, many fielders can learn to anticipate where the ball will be hit. As fielders play the field regularly they get a good feel of how hard a ball has been hit and which fielders the ball might be coming to. This can take time, though. Everyone's reaction times are different, and they tend to improve through the teenage years. Plus some physiques are better built for diving and being thrown about.

The first skill to learn in fielding is stopping the ball. If players can't stop and collect the ball properly, they will be surely ineffective in the field. There are two ways to collect the cricket ball that should be taught: at the centre of the body and on the side of the body.

Collecting the Ball in the Centre of the Body

The ball can be collected in the centre of the body by assuming a position called the long barrier, which is achieved by attacking the ball so that the ball comes toward the centre of the body (figure 7.1a). If a player is right-handed, she will kneel with her left knee so her entire left leg is sideways to the ball to form a "long barrier," which is how this method got its name (figure 7.1b). By keeping eyes on the ball and placing hands in front of the knee, fielders can collect the ball comfortably and then stand up to throw it. If the ball is missed with the hands, it will be stopped by the leg or other body part rather than go for extra runs.

Collecting the Ball on the Left or Right Side

The next way to stop a cricket ball is when the fielder is attacking the ball and running onto it. Figure 7.2 shows how a fielder comes in to the ball when it is on the throwing side of the body. This is so the player can collect the ball and throw in one movement. The fielder's head is steady, body low, and hands in a position to give a good-sized target for picking the ball up cleanly. Note that the fielder's foot plants in line with the ball as an extra backup in case the ball should jump or bobble. The ball would then be stopped by the foot. Once

Figure 7.1 Collecting the ball in the centre of the body using the "long barrier" method.

Figure 7.2 Collecting the ball on the throwing side of the body.

cleanly collected, the ball can be thrown as usual in one clean movement, ensuring a fast, accurate throw to the wicket keeper.

If a fielder must collect a ball from the non-throwing side of the body, as shown in figure 7.3, it's important to get into position as early as possible when moving into the ball. However, there might be times when it's not possible to turn into position in time because the ball is coming too fast to the fielder's nonthrowing side. This is when collection of the ball must take place on this "wrong" side. In this case, the fielder tries to get the nonthrowing side foot in line with the ball and make a collection before transferring the ball into the throwing hand and taking a moment to turn into

Coaching Tip

As with most fielding basics, you want to try to keep things simple. Make sure fielders watch the ball into both hands, not just one hand. Keeping the body low when attacking is important to ensure a clean collection. Fielders can throw the ball only after they have picked it up, so taking time to practice collecting balls correctly will help with run outs.

Figure 7.3   Collecting the ball on the nonthrowing side of the body.

a normal throwing position. As long as collection of a cricket ball cleanly on the nonthrowing side is made safely, it cannot be wrong. The art of fielding is to gather the ball cleanly, and different players have their own way of doing so.

Catching the Ball

One of the most destructive things in cricket is when a catch is dropped. This is the football equivalent of scoring an own goal. No one ever intends to drop a catch, but it happens, and sometimes in the worst of situations. Even at the international level, matches are lost and series decided by spilt catches. Catching should never be taken for granted and must constantly be worked on.

As coach, it's your duty to teach your young players great technique so that when their opportunity in the field comes they have a far better chance of success. Remember that young players have softer hands than adults and the ball stings them more. This is why some youngsters are reluctant to try to catch a fast-moving ball or a high skyer that comes down with snow on it.

Coaching Tip

Many young players don't open their hands properly for catches and thus get hit on the fingers, which can put them off fielding. If your team is young or inexperienced, work on catching with tennis balls or "slaz" balls (harder tennis balls) that don't hurt the hands so much but allow you to train the techniques of catching.

Start slow, and build up to high catches and hard-hit balls. Most catches at the junior level will not be massive steepling catches that disappear into the clouds. They are most likely to be 15- to 20-metre (about 50- to 65-foot) catches in the infield. You should practice what players are most likely to get.

Catching the ball is done by cupping the hands and presenting as large a surface area to the ball as possible. This is achieved by the small fingers touching at the sides of the palms of each hand. For below-the-waist catches (such as slips) the fingers will point down (figure 7.4). For high catches in front of the body or diving catches, the fingers

Figure 7.4   Catching the ball below the waist.

will point forward (figure 7.5). For catches around chest height and above, the fingers will point skyward—also known as reverse hands (figure 7.6). This helps fielders decide on the correct setup with their hands. In reverse hands catching, the index fingers and thumbs overlap and the fingers point upward. This style of catching is especially popular in Australia and South Africa when fielders are unsure which way to set their hands up for high catches.

a   b

Figure 7.5   Catching the ball in front of the body.

a   b

Figure 7.6   Catching the ball at chest height and above.

In catching, one of the most important factors is balance. It is harder to catch when everything is moving about, so arriving underneath the ball, or directly in the line of the ball with the body, is key to being able to balance and stay steady underneath a catch. Finally, the hands should "give" a little as the ball is taken to decelerate the ball speed. Give also helps avoid "hard hands" from which the ball can bounce out.

Slip Catching

Like any close-to-the-wicket position, slip fielding is a specialist position. It's worthwhile finding out who on your team has a good pair of catching hands and is able to catch at slip. Players need good reactions and excellent levels of concentration to field close to the batsman because any and every ball could come their way in a game. This means they should expect every ball and always be prepared to react quickly.

The basic body position for a slip fielder requires "soft knees," with the player in a relaxed stance with relaxed shoulders and hands out slightly in front of the body at around knee height (figure 7.7). Body weight should be on the balls of the feet and body position fairly low to make it easier to spring upward than to go down and take a catch.

A slip fielder will quickly learn to determine the correct position of the hands to meet the line of the ball. But far and away the most important thing for a slip fielder is to watch the edge of the bat (if they are a close first slip, they can watch the ball like a wicket keeper). Anticipation and expectation mean more to a close fielder than anything else. If they expect every ball to come to them, they will not be surprised when it does.

Figure 7.7   Body position for slip fielder.

Throwing the Ball

Although many cricketers don't know how to properly throw a ball, the teaching of throwing is relatively simple. The importance of a good throw cannot be overstated. Run outs at the junior level account for a higher percentage of dismissals than those at senior level. And this is because of a lack of understanding between batsmen when judging runs. Players throwing with accuracy is a joy for any coach to watch. Accurate throws make a team look disciplined and professional, and they really help out the wicket keeper, who, let's face it, has a thankless task at best.

If you have inexperienced players on your team, tell them this: The easiest way to get a round of applause from teammates and those watching is a good, accurate throw. They will then feel part of the game and instantly a part of the team. A pinpoint return from the outfield to the wicket keeper is worthy of acclaim at any level of the game. So let's look at the two types of throws used in cricket: the infield throw and the outfield throw.

Infield Throw

The infield throw is designed to release the ball fast, and sometimes with little time to set the position correctly. But, in figure 7.8, we show the correct positioning. Note that the throwing arm comes up into an L shape to line up the throwing shoulder with the target. It's the throwing shoulder that dictates how accurate the throw is going to be, so we want to ensure the shoulder drives toward the target on the throw itself. The fielder's weight transfers from back leg to front leg, and the arm pulls through and extends to release the ball. The fielder's weight then steps forward to maintain balance.

a   b   c

Figure 7.8 Infield throw.

Outfield Throw

The outfield throw differs from the infield throw in one main respect: The throwing arm is fully elongated before the throw is made, as shown in figure 7.9. This is to stretch the arm (like a bow and arrow) and create longer levers. Notice that the knuckles of the hand face upward; this helps keep the throwing elbow up in the throw rather than down below the throwing shoulder. When throwing for distance, good form is better than power because correct technique allows all your energy to flow through the ball. This is also why it's important to ensure weight transfer from back to front foot and to have a good step or drive out of the throwing action.

a   b

c   d

Figure 7.9   Outfield throw.

Crow Hop

The crow hop is a small step before the ball is thrown that helps players line up to the target and get good balance. The hop is effectively a little skip that creates a stepping movement so that the thrower's power can be driven from the throwing side. The crow hop allows a spilt-second for throwers to set themselves and helps with creating good throwing form.

After fielding the ball (figure 7.10a), the player kicks up the back leg and passes it in front of the other leg, turning it sideways before it hits the ground (figure 7.10b). He points his lead shoulder and hip at the target to align his body for the throw. Once his foot lands, he maintains momentum by stepping forward and throwing the ball (figure 7.10c). His follow-through brings his throwing arm over his lead leg as the back foot rises off the ground from behind.

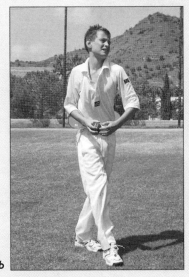

Figure 7.10 Crow hop.

Fielding Drills

Effective drills are pointed and efficient. You'll see that our fielding drills focus on the key points we have discussed in the chapter and are designed to make every second count. Be as creative as you can in modifying these drills to suit the needs of your players.

For each drill you'll find an objective for the drill, the equipment you'll need, the organization and setup, instructions for how to run the drill, the technique you are looking for, and how to make the drill either easier or harder to match the age and skill level of your players. The skill should be self-explanatory and useful in assisting you with coaching technique and method. Also check out Appendix C: 15 Game-Based Drills on page 175.

All-Around Fielding

Objectives: To improve and develop ground fielding skills; to improve speed of return; to focus on accuracy and teach confidence in collecting and releasing the ball

What You'll Need: 6 or more players, 3 cones, 1 ball, 2 stumps

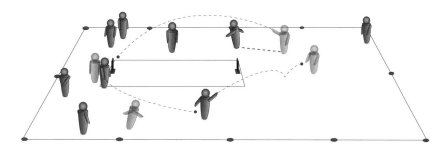

Procedure: Groups of players are organised as shown. The coach rolls the ball to the left of the player positioned at the cone to his right. The player executes a pickup and an underarm throw return. The coach then rolls the ball into the channel for the player positioned at the cone in front of him to chase, pick up, and throw at a set of stumps. The player positioned at the cone to the coach's left then moves to back up this throw and returns it to the second player, who has moved behind the stumps. The second player then turns and throws the ball to the coach. After each throw, players move counterclockwise one station. After receiving the ball, the coach rolls the ball out for the next group of players to repeat the exercise. The drill continues until all players have repeated each skill a set number of times.

Key Points
- Approach each ball in a balanced, aggressive manner with head still and eyes level.
- Assess the position of the ball early and adopt a line slightly to the non-throwing side of the ball. Pick the ball up outside of the throwing foot, keeping the head steady and watching the ball into the hand.
- Follow through after the throw in the direction of the target.
- When backing up a throw, get behind the line of the ball as quickly as possible.

Variations: To increase difficulty, increase the distance between the coach and players; increase the distance players have to move; use a one-handed pickup and throw with the nondominant hand; use smaller targets, such as a small box; add a competitive element, such as the player with the most hits is the winner; use hard balls, such as proper cricket balls. To decrease difficulty, reduce the distance between the coach and players; reduce the distance players have to move; use bigger targets (e.g., a full set of stumps); use lighter balls, such as tennis balls.

Close Catching

Objectives: To acquire and develop close and high catching skills; to select and apply catching skills according to height and pace of the ball; to improve close and high catching skills by watching how other players catch the ball and evaluating what parts of the skill they need to use to improve their catching technique

What You'll Need: 8 players or more, 5 cones, 12 tennis balls

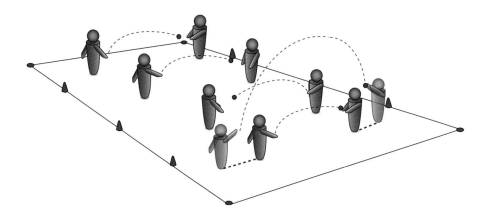

Procedure: Players work in pairs in two straight lines about 3 to 5 metres (about 10 to 16 feet) apart (or 5 to 10 metres [16 to 32 feet] apart for high catching) as shown. One player throws a ball underarm to a partner to practice catching.

Key Points
- Stand relaxed with feet about shoulder-width apart, knees bent, and weight on the balls of the feet.
- Hands are together with fingers pointing down or, for high catches, hands together with palms facing the ball. Make a big catching area.
- Head is level and eyes are on the ball.
- "Give" with the ball.

Variations: Increase throwing distance; vary direction and height; add another ball; use a bigger ball; play Distraction Catching, as described on page 82, a game in which players see how many catches they can make in a set amount of time; catch one-handed.

Two-Handed Intercept and Throw

Objectives: To acquire and develop intercepting and overarm throwing skills; to select and apply intercepting and throwing skills depending on the pace of serve and length of required throw; to evaluate performance by observing others and listening to and understanding instruction; to improve performance by identifying areas to focus on when performing the skill

What You'll Need: 4 or more players in pairs, 1 tennis ball per pair

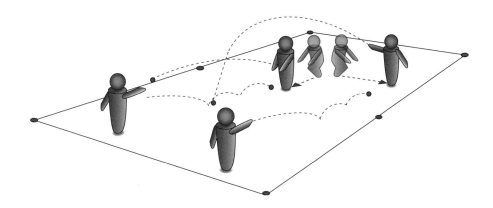

Procedure: In pairs, as shown, one player rolls the ball out about two thirds the distance of the playing area. Her partner attacks the ball on the bounce, picks the ball up with two hands, and then overarm throws the ball back to her partner. Repeat five times, then players change over.

Key Points
- Attack the ball by getting low early and maintaining balance.
- Keep the head steady and eyes on the ball.
- Pick up ball central to the body and ensure the body is sideways when the ball is picked up. Pick up the ball with two hands.
- Adopt the correct throwing position, using a crow hop if necessary, and follow through to the target.

Variations: Increase or decrease throwing distance; increase or decrease pace of serve; approach from different angles; use a stationary ball; use a different ball; use a crow hop if throwing from a distance; use stumps as a target; include running batters.

Distraction Catching

Objectives: To acquire and develop close catching skills by adding distractions during catching; to select and apply skills and tactics to catch the ball effectively and ignore distractions; to improve performance by listening to instructions, watching other participants perform the skill, and making a judgment on how they are performing to improve their catching technique

What You'll Need: Players in groups of 4, 4 cones per group; 1 tennis ball for every two players

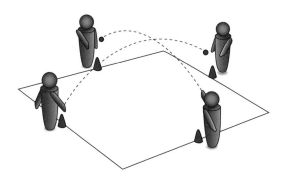

Procedure: In groups of four, players form a square, as shown; two players have a ball. Players with balls throw the ball underarm to their partner (the player directly across the square) to practice close catching. Other balls are distractions as they cross in midair.

Key Points
- Stand relaxed with feet about shoulder-width apart, knees bent, and weight on the balls of the feet.
- Hands are together with fingers pointing down, making a big catching area.
- Head is level and eyes are on the ball.
- "Give" with the ball.

Variations: Increase throwing distance; vary direction and height; add another ball per pair; use a bigger ball; time the game to see how many catches each player can make; catch one-handed.

Turnabout Catching

Objectives: To acquire and develop close catching skills under pressure by turning around to receive a catch; to select and apply skills by ensuring the catcher has turned around fully before the ball is received; to evaluate performance by listening to instruction and observing other participants; to use self-analysis to improve areas of deficiency when catching

What You'll Need: Players in groups of 3; 2 tennis balls per group

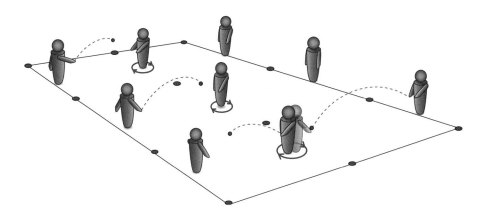

Procedure: In groups of three, as shown, one player throws the ball to the player in the middle, who then returns it back. The player in the middle quickly turns around to receive a catch from the other player behind him. The player in the middle returns the ball and then turns around again. This repeats for a set number of repetitions or time. Give all players a turn in the middle.

Key Points
- Stand relaxed with feet about shoulder-width apart, knees bent, and weight on balls of feet to make for quick turns.
- Hands are together with fingers pointing down, making a big catching area.
- Head is level and eyes are on the ball.
- "Give" with the ball.

Variations: Increase throwing distance; vary direction and height; use bigger balls; time the game to see how many catches each player can make; catch one-handed; use diving catches; use overarm throws.

Pairs Target Barrier

Objectives: To acquire and develop the skill of stopping the ball using a long barrier technique; to select and apply tactics to try to score points and prevent a partner from scoring points; to evaluate and improve performance by observing partner's performance, listening to instruction, and analysing in which ways they can improve to prevent the ball from passing

What You'll Need: 8 players in pairs, 1 tennis ball per pair, 4 cones per pair

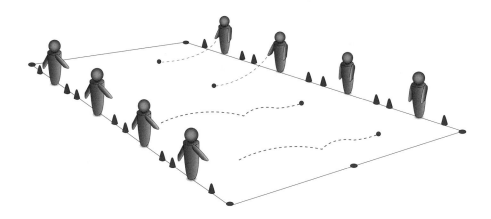

Procedure: Players in pairs, as shown, try to score points by rolling the ball underarm at their partner's goals. Goals are about 2 metres (6.5 feet) apart. Players use the long barrier method when stopping the ball. Continue for a set amount of time or until a designated score has been achieved.

Key Points

- Adopt the ready position, which is a relaxed stance with weight slightly forward and on the balls of the feet.
- Go down on knee opposite the throwing arm; the back foot rests behind the front knee to form a wedge, so the body is positioned at a right angle to the ball.
- Keep the head over the ball and eyes on the ball.
- Fingers point down.

Variations: Increase or decrease the throwing distance; increase or decrease the size of goals; use different size or different shaped balls; perform the long barrier on the opposite side.

Many Skill Fielding

Objectives: To acquire and develop a range of fielding skills under pressure; to select and apply skills according to the type of delivery, distance, and pace players are receiving it; to evaluate performance by observing partner's performance, listening to instruction, and self-analysing to identify areas to improve

What You'll Need: Players in groups of 2, 2 or 3 tennis balls per group (semi-hard or hard balls may be used depending on group ability), 2 cones per group; 1 set of stumps per group

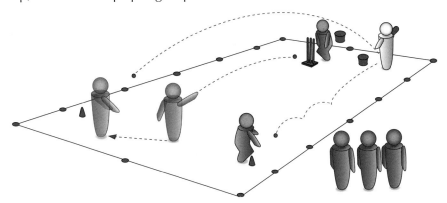

Procedure: Players are in groups of two, as shown. The coach hits a high ball for the fielder to move to the left to catch and then throw back to the wicket keeper. As the fielder throws the ball back, the coach rolls a slower ball for the fielder to attack and then underarm throw to the keeper. If preferred, have the fielder run around the coach and back into the channel, whereby the coach hits a further ball over the fielder's shoulder for another catch and throw to the wicket keeper. Once complete, restart the drill with a new pair of players.

Key Points
- When catching, watch the ball; keep head steady; hands stay together; give with the ball; fingers either point down or up, depending on the type of catch.
- When intercepting, attack the ball; keep low and in line when approaching the ball; watch the ball into the hand.
- When throwing underarm, pick up and throw underarm in a rhythmical motion; follow through toward the target; keep head steady throughout.
- When throwing overarm, hold the ball across its seam; maintain a balanced, wide base; the elbow of the front arm points at target; the throwing elbow is level with the shoulder as it comes through; the back leg trails until after the release; follow through.

Variations: Increase or decrease the catching distance; increase or decrease the pace of the serve; pick up the ball with the weaker hand; use different types of balls; use a bigger ball.

Retrieve and Throw

Objectives: To acquire and develop retrieving and throwing skills under pressure; to select and apply retrieving and throwing skills according to pace of delivery and distance; to evaluate and improve retrieving and throwing skills by observing others, listening to and following instructions, and identifying areas that to be improved

What You'll Need: 8 players in pairs, 1 tennis ball per pair, 3 cones to separate pairs

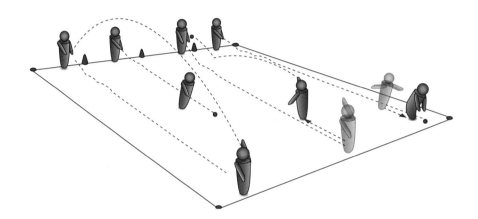

Procedure: Players work in pairs, as shown; both players in each pair start at the end of the playing area with the cones. One partner rolls out the ball across the area, and her partner must chase and retrieve the ball, turn, and throw overarm back to her partner from the far baseline of the playing area. Repeat three or four times before switching roles.

Key Points
- Chase the ball aggressively and assume a low body position when approaching the ball.
- Make sure to be level with the ball before picking it up.
- Balance remains central on the pickup.
- Pick up level with outside of throwing foot for short retrieve; pick up level with inside of throwing foot for long retrieve.
- Turn the opposite way to throwing arm, adopt throwing position, and throw.

Variations: Increase or decrease retrieving distance; increase or decrease speed of serve; approach ball from the throwing and nonthrowing sides of the body; use a stationary ball.

One-Handed Intercept

Objectives: To acquire and develop intercepting and underarm throwing skills; to select and apply intercepting and throwing skills depending on pace of delivery and length of throw; to evaluate performance by observing others and listening to and understanding instruction; to improve performance by identifying areas to focus on when performing the skill

What You'll Need: 4 players in pairs, 1 tennis ball per pair

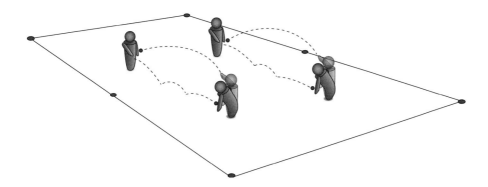

Procedure: In pairs, as shown, one partner rolls the ball out to the halfway point. The partner attacks the ball and throws the ball underarm (no bounce) back. Repeat five times, and then players change.

Key Points
- Attack the ball and get low early.
- Maintain balance and watch the ball.
- Pick up the ball on your throwing side.
- Throwing hand arm and body follow through to target.

Variations: Increase or decrease throwing distance; increase or decrease speed of serve; use a stationary ball; use weak hand; use different balls; add stumps; use batters running between the wickets.

Coaching Wicket Keeping

Wicket keeping is the most individual of positions in cricket—a one of a kind on the team. But it is worth letting all of your young players try this position because some are naturally gifted and many might not get the opportunity very often. The secret to being a good wicket keeper is anticipation. It's often very hard for a young wicket keeper to watch the ball and retain focus on it without being distracted by anything else the batsman is doing. This is why anticipation, expectation, and preparation to catch every ball are the hallmarks of a good keeper.

> **Coaching Tip**
>
> The most difficult thing for a young keeper to try to do is stay down until the ball has pitched. Many want to stand up early, but this means that if the ball stays low or does something odd, they won't be able to take it cleanly. So get them to stay down until the ball pitches. It takes practice as well as belief in their abilities.

A wicket keeper should be relaxed in the arms but have explosive legs, so balance and footwork are vital components. Soft hands (not going too hard at the ball), excellent movement, and high levels of concentration are the remaining skills you hope to have in your keeper. The best wicket keepers somehow make their gloves look like giant cushions. They "give" with the ball and keep their hands together to form as large an area as possible for the ball to nestle into. Some say that poor wicket keepers must dive a lot. This must mean that if keepers have great footwork, they probably don't need to dive very often.

Wicket keepers maintain a crouched position to keep a level view. Their start position is close to the height of the ball they are likely to catch. This helps them to keep watching the ball and allows them to rest their hands on the ground in case the ball doesn't bounce very much. Different wicket keepers crouch in different ways, but the ideal position is for the body weight to be on the balls of the feet so the keeper looks like a downhill skier, as shown in figure 7.11. The wicket keeper's head and eyes are level, and weight is evenly distributed on each foot. The fingers of the gloves are just touching the ground, and the arms are relaxed, almost monkey like.

Wicket keepers must be able to see the ball at all times. They will stand just outside off stump and, when standing up, their chin will be level to the height of the ball (figure 7.12a). When standing back, the keeper is aiming to take the ball at waist height (figure 7.12b).

The catching techniques we covered in fielding apply to wicket keepers, so the glove work should be similar. The main difference is that a wicket keeper should expect every ball and is likely to be at the centre of any fielding performance. This means that if any mistakes are made, there's no time to dwell on them. A keeper is going to take the vast majority of balls in an innings, either directly from the bowler of via a fielder throwing to the stumps. So a young keeper cannot afford to lose concentration but should remain upbeat and focused at all times.

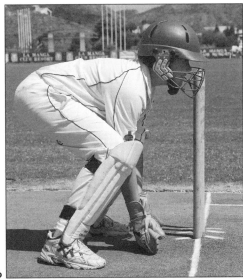

Figure 7.11   Basic crouching body position for a wicket keeper: *(a)* front view and *(b)* side view.

Figure 7.12   Wicket keeper *(a)* standing up and *(b)* standing back.

Wicket keeping is a key position for any team. Following are some drills and pointers for wannabe keepers and others who would like to have a go. It never hurts for all members of a team to try out wicket keeping so they realise how tough a job it can be.

Standing Up

Objectives: To acquire and develop the skill of wicket keeping when standing up to the stumps; to select and apply skills when standing up to the stumps according to line and height of the ball; to evaluate and improve performance by listening to and following instructions and identifying areas to improve on.

What You'll Need: 4 players in pairs, 1 cone per pair, 1 tennis ball per pair, 1 set of stumps per pair

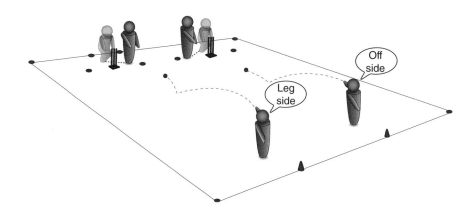

Procedure: Players work in pairs, as shown, one partner feeding the ball with one bounce (off side to begin) to a partner who is acting as wicket keeper. Repeat for a set number of goes on the leg side. Then change the delivery, alternating deliveries as the practice progresses. Players rotate after a set number of repetitions or a set time.

Key Points
- Begin from a crouched position slightly to off side with feet about shoulder-width apart and weight on the balls of the feet.
- Head is steady; eyes are fixed on the ball.
- Come up with the bounce with hands together and fingers pointing down, making a big surface catching area.
- Hips and body rotate to allow for high-rising balls.
- Give with the ball.

Variations: Increase or decrease the throwing distance; vary the length of the serve; vary the pace of the serve; use a bigger ball; add distractions; add a batter; use different balls.

Standing Back

Objectives: To acquire and develop the skill of wicket keeping when standing back; to select and apply skills when standing back according to line, pace, and height of the ball; to evaluate and improve performance by listening to and following instructions and identifying areas to improve

What You'll Need: 4 players in pairs, 1 cone per pair, 1 tennis ball per pair, 1 set of stumps per pair

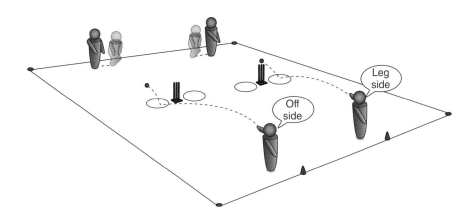

Procedure: Players work in pairs, as shown, with one player feeding the ball with one bounce (off side to begin) in the area next to the stump (see rings on either side of the stump in the illustration) to his partner who is acting as wicket keeper. Repeat for a set number of goes on the leg side. Then change the delivery, alternating deliveries as the practice progresses. Players rotate after a set number of repetitions or a set time.

Key Points
- Begin from a crouched position slightly to off side with feet about shoulder-width apart and weight on the balls of the feet.
- Head is steady; eyes are fixed on the ball.
- Just as the ball starts to dip, come up with the bounce with hands together and fingers pointing down, making a big surface catching area.
- Hips and body rotate to allow for high-rising balls.
- Give with the ball.

Variations: Increase or decrease the throwing distance; vary the length of the serve; vary the pace of the serve; use a bigger ball; add distractions; add a batter; use different balls.

Wicket Keeper Diving

Objectives: To acquire and develop the skill of wicket keeping diving; to select and apply skills when wicket keeping diving according to line and height of the ball; to evaluate and improve performance by listening to and following instructions and identifying areas to improve on; to understand the benefits of being fit by continually squatting and then diving to receive the ball

What You'll Need: A group of 4 players, 1 cone per group, 1 basket of tennis balls per group

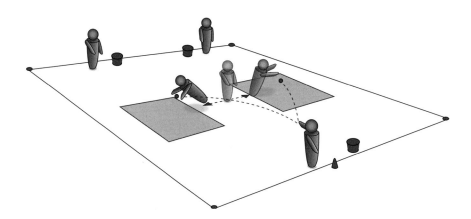

Procedure: Working in groups, as shown, the first player feeds the ball with one bounce (off side to begin) to the player in the middle, who is acting as wicket keeper. Repeat for a set number of goes on the leg side. The other two players stand at the far end of the playing area to catch balls that get past the player in the middle. Deliveries can be alternated as the practice progresses. Players rotate after a set number of repetitions or a set time. Note that where the ground or floor is firm, mats should always be used as shown in the illustration; the mat might not be necessary for outdoor work on grass if the ground is soft.

Key Points
- Begin from a crouched position slightly to off side with feet about shoulder-width apart and weight on the balls of the feet.
- Head is steady; eyes are fixed on the ball.
- Come up with the bounce with hands together, making a big surface catching area.
- Dive flat and roll with the ball.
- Give with the ball.

Variations: Increase or decrease the throwing distance; vary the length of the serve; vary the pace of the serve; use a bigger ball; add distractions; add a batter; use different balls; catch one-handed.

Three-Player Diamond

Objectives: To acquire and develop the skill of wicket keeping; to select and apply skills when wicket keeping according to line and height of the ball; to evaluate and improve performance by listening to and following instructions and identifying areas to improve on; to understand the benefits of being fit by continually squatting to receive the ball

What You'll Need: Players in groups of 3, 3 cones per group, 1 tennis ball per group

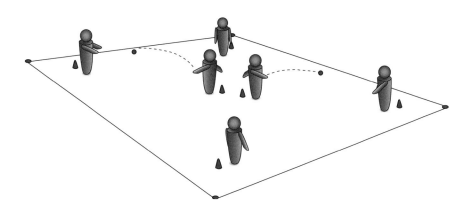

Procedure: Working in groups of three, as shown, one player feeds the ball underarm to either of the other two players in the group. The recipient must initially adopt a crouched position before the ball is thrown. Repeated for a set number of goes or a set time. Alternate deliveries as the practice progresses (high serve, low serve, direct, low bounce, high bounce). Players rotate after a set number of goes.

Key Points
- Begin from a crouched position with feet about shoulder-width apart and weight on the balls of the feet.
- Head is steady; eyes are fixed on the ball.
- Come up with the bounce with hands together and fingers pointing down, making a big surface catching area.
- Hips and body rotate to allow for high rising ball.
- Give with the ball.

Variations: Increase or decrease the throwing distance; vary the length of the serve; vary the pace of the serve; use a bigger ball; add distractions; add a batter; use different balls; catch one-handed.

Coaching Bowling

8

Most coaches will know from experience that bowling is not the most popular skill for coaches to teach their young students. This might have something to do with beginning coaches being uncomfortable coaching a skill they are not so great at themselves. But whether you're a skilled bowler yourself or not, your players need to learn to execute the finer points of bowling if they are to develop as cricket players. Bowling is a very important facet of the game.

Established bowlers have titles based on their particular skill sets in bowling. Fast bowlers bowl with pace, spin bowlers turn the ball with all their might, and swing bowlers, as you might expect, put a swing on the cricket ball. You'll need to discover who on your team has the ability to bowl fast, who can spin, and who can swing because you want to encourage and work toward a bowler's speciality. It might be worth encouraging players who have never bowled before to have a go at it as well. History tells us that many a decent bowler has been discovered by getting a nonbowler to have a go in nets only to find they have a hidden natural talent for bowling.

So it's worth teaching batsmen who simply want to bat all the time the value of decent bowling practice by getting them to bowl. Before players begin to specialise too much, you might find some bowlers might be able to bowl both spin and pace equally. It's always worthwhile taking time to find out who can do what, much like discovering a defender who turns out to be a world-class striker in football. This is what happened to Theirry Henry at Arsenal, for example. Keep an open mind at youth cricket level. You might just find a diamond in the rough. Also, if you're just getting started as a coach, know that there are simple things you can do and still come across as a knowledgeable coach. Part of coaching a skill as complex as bowling is to keep instruction simple. Once your bowlers understand what they are doing, they'll be able to help themselves.

Basic Bowling Concepts

The secret of being a good bowler is to have a consistent bowling action that you can repeat under all conditions. This results in having control over where the ball goes, which of course is vital if you want to build up pressure on a batting side and take wickets, as well as keep runs down.

Coaches refer to bowling a "line and length," which refers to where the ball lands just around off stump (line) and about 2 or 3 metres (2.1 to 3.2 yards) in front of the batsman (length). This makes the ball harder to hit because the range of shots a batsman can play is drastically reduced. The likely shot choice is a defensive one. You would imagine as a bowler that there is no batsman at all and that the ball will go on to hit the top of the off stump. Ideally, this is what any good bowler is trying to do. When a ball lands in this area it also has a chance to move off the pitch or in the air, making it even harder for the batsman to deal with the delivery. Much of the practice for young bowlers thus consists of trying to control how and where they release the ball to ensure it lands where they want it to more often than not.

As a coach, you'll have to teach the basics of the bowling action in addition to encouraging your players to understand more about the finer points, which will include bowling variations, slower balls, and being able to change the length bowled to stop the batsman playing different types of shots. Learning how and when to change what a bowler does is part of the experience of learning the game.

Line

Line refers to bowling straight (at off stump). Encourage your bowlers to run up straight, go through the crease straight, and follow through straight. Then the ball will usually go straight. If you keep it that simple, most bowlers will not try to do anything awkward with their body positions. Bowlers often forget these basics and develop a bowling action that makes it harder to be consistent and accurate.

Length

Length is simply when you let the ball go. Hang on to the ball too long, and it's short; let the ball go too early, and it's too full. So a bowler is effectively looking to give a high-five to the batsman to effect an ideal release point. Bowling with a perfect release point is a skill in itself, similar to hitting a tennis ball consistently well when serving. But through trial and error and feeling the release point, young bowlers can begin to understand when to let the ball go

Coaching the Basics of Bowling

When teaching bowling to young players, start with the four tent peg approach, named as such because these are the four things in the bowling action that are not negotiable—a bit like using four pegs to keep a tent stable and secure. Figure 8.1 shows the full bowling action, which we will further break down into each of the tent pegs. This will give you an idea of the sequencing and the key points to focus on to ensure your bowlers have repeatable actions.

Figure 8.1   Ideal bowling action.

Tent Peg 1

The first tent peg is back-foot impact. This is the moment that a bowler's back leg impacts in the action, as shown in figure 8.1a. The idea is for the back leg to be stable and support the whole movement, which requires no leaning back but being relaxed and upright.

Once the back foot impacts at this point, any other part of the body can move *except* the back foot, so you'll need to look at which way this foot points. If the back foot runs parallel with the crease, this is known as having a sideways setup. If the foot points at 45 degrees (toward the square leg umpire), this is known as having a midway or semi-setup. If the back foot lands pointing straight down the pitch, this is known as having a front-on setup. This is all very important to know as a coach and as a player because the rest of the action depends on that back foot's position. That is, the bowler's hips and shoulders will be at the same angle and not split apart on tent peg 1 because this would create a mixed action that might lead to injuries and line-up problems.

When bowlers are in the tent peg 1 position, their bowling hand is in line with their bowling shoulder, and their front knee is in line with their elbow, lifting the knee up as if attached by string. This ensures shoulders and hips line up correctly. They should be balanced and relaxed with all body weight supported on the back leg.

Tent Peg 2

The second tent peg is front-foot impact. It's against the front foot and leg that a bowler pulls to create drive and speed. In the tent peg 2 position, the bowler looks like a five-point star or an X shape, with hands as far apart as possible (to create a stretch) and the balance of weight equally between each foot, as shown in figure 8.1b. The feeling for a young player might be that of grabbing the batsman's collar with the leading hand and grabbing the sightscreen from behind with the other. The position is a power position in a straight line.

Tent Peg 3

The third tent peg is release of the cricket ball. The body leans forward, and the bowler feels as though he or she is giving a high-five with the bowling hand lined up with the bowling hip and in front of the front foot, as shown in figure 8.1c. The hips and chest face the batsman, and again the release is balanced, with everything moving toward the target.

Tent Peg 4

The fourth and final tent peg is the follow-through. The body drives forward, and the trailing leg drives hard toward the batsman to bring the hips through, as shown in figure 8.1d. The arms rotate fully, and the top half drives forward.

The four tent peg approach helps young bowlers understand where they ought to be at any one time. After going over and demonstrating the four pegs, have your bowlers try to put all the positions together in one flowing movement. Once they can do it, they have achieved full bowling action. In practice, have your bowlers walk up to the crease, step into tent peg 1, and flow through their bowling action. Also have them *run* up to the crease, jump into tent peg 1, and bowl with a flowing motion. By using the four tent peg approach, you reinforce that bowlers are aware of these important positions.

Gripping the Ball

Bowlers grip a cricket ball in several ways, but some are better than others if you want to land the ball on its seam. And that's what bowlers, whether fast or spin, are trying to do. When the ball hits the seam, it deviates off the pitch, making it difficult for a batsman to play. If the ball is spinning hard, the seam adds to the grip on the pitch and makes it turn more. An upright seam also assists with the swing of a cricket ball. Let's now review a few of the basic grips.

Seam Bowler

The grip for the seam bowler, shown in figure 8.2, requires the index finger and middle finger to be on either side of the seam. The thumb is on the side of the ball near the underneath, or on the seam itself, and the ring finger and little finger are bent and resting on the side of the ball. The ball is held in the pads of the fingers, not gripped too tightly—more like holding an egg.

Figure 8.2   Seam bowler grip.

When this ball is bowled it spins backward and leaves the middle finger last. The wrist flicks forward, giving the feeling of playing with a yo-yo. It's this backward spin that helps the ball stay upright and more likely to hit the seam. Figure 8.3 shows a release using the seam bowler grip.

Swing Bowler

The grip for the swing bowler is the same as the grip for the seam bowler: the index finger and middle finger on either side of the seam and the thumb resting underneath the ball, either on the seam or on the leather. The ring finger and little finger rest on the side of the ball (figure 8.4). But for the swing bowler grip the seam is angled the way the bowler wants the ball to swing. The shiniest side of the ball should always face the batsman. Then simply turning the seam to a 20- to 30-degree angle makes it act something like a rudder through the air. Hold it at that angle as for the seam bowler grip, and bowl normally. Don't "try" to swing the ball or it might end up as a push.

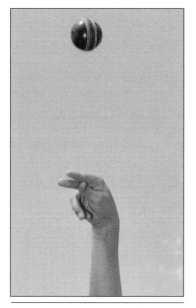

Figure 8.3 Release using the seam bowler grip.

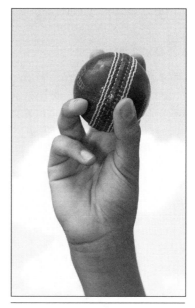

Figure 8.4 Swing bowler grip.

Off Spin

The grip for the off spin requires the player to hold the ball across the seam with the index and middle finger spread apart so that the ball is gripped by the knuckles of the fingers, as shown in figure 8.5. The remaining grip is the same as for seam bowling, with the ring finger and little finger resting on the side of the ball.

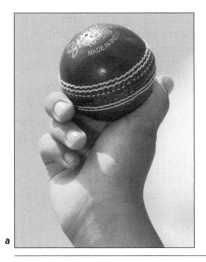

a

b

Figure 8.5   Off-spin grip.

When the ball is bowled, the bowler turns the hand over, similar to opening a round door knob, and the fingers rip down the right side of the ball (for a right-handed bowler). This adds revolutions on the ball, which is what makes it turn. The more "revs" on the ball, the more the ball turns. Figure 8.6 shows a release using the off-spin grip.

Leg Spin

In the leg spin grip, the bowler holds the ball across the seam with the index and middle finger spread not so far apart as for the off-spin delivery, as shown in figure 8.7. The remaining grip is the same as for seam bowling, with the ring finger and little finger resting on the side of the ball.

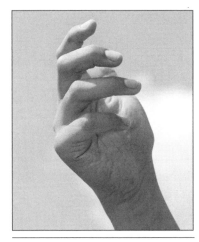

Figure 8.6   Release using the off-spin grip.

Figure 8.7   Leg spin grip.

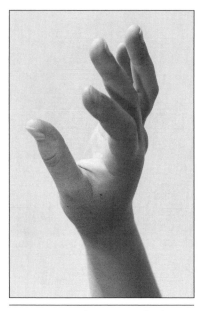

When the ball is bowled. the bowler turns the wrist from the leg side to the off side (a bit like washing a window or waving at someone), and the ring finger rolls over the ball to create additional revolutions and make it spin. The palm of the bowler's hand faces the batsman on release of the ball to create maximum turn (figure 8.8).

Figure 8.8 Release using the leg spin grip.

Bowling Drills

In the drills that follow you can use focus on proper execution of the key points discussed in this chapter. Modify the drills as necessary for your team.

For each drill, you'll find the objectives of the drill, the equipment you'll need, the organization and setup, instructions on how to run the drill, the technique you're looking for, and how to make the drill either easier or harder, depending on the ages and skill levels of your players. Also check out Appendix C: 15 Game-Based Drills on page 175.

Bowling Action

Objectives: To acquire and develop the skill of bowling by observing the coach bowl and then trying to copy the technique and evaluate performance by watching how other players bowl, identifying problem areas to improve on

What You'll Need: 6 players in pairs, 2 cones per pair, 1 tennis ball per pair

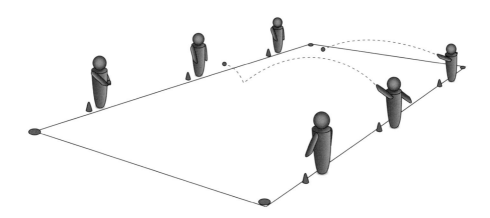

Procedure: Players bowl in pairs, as shown. One player bowls the ball to a partner from 10 to 20 metres (32 to 65 feet) apart, depending on age. Players initially bowl from a base position. Partners change roles after a set number of goes.

Key Points

- Use a basic grip with thumb on the seam and index and middle finger on either side of the seam.
- Assume a strong base position with hips and shoulders in line, weight forward, and hands gathered in front of face.
- Take a comfortable stride toward the target in which the front arm pushes out toward the target, the bowling hand pushes out and down, the arms swing fully, the shoulders rotate, and the back leg steps through.
- Head is steady.

Variations: Change to front on, side on, or midway action; bowl underarm; vary distance; progress to run up and bowl.

Bowling Relay

Objectives: To acquire and develop the skill of bowling under competition; to select and apply bowling skills to effectively bowl straight and efficiently between designated cones; for players to evaluate their own bowling by watching others, listening to instructions, and applying what they have observed to perfecting their own technique

What You'll Need: Players in two groups of 5, 1 tennis ball per group, 6 cones per group, 1 set of stumps per group

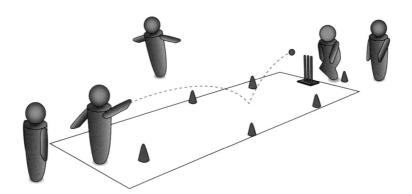

Procedure: The first player in line behind the cone bowls down a channel between two sets of cones to the player behind the stumps, who acts as the wicket keeper. The wicket keeper fields the ball and then bowls back to the next player in line behind the cone and runs to the end of the opposite line while the player bowls the ball back to the next wicket keeper in line. Continue until all players return to their starting position.

Key Points
- Keep head level and steady.
- Assume a strong base position with hips and shoulders in line throughout the delivery.
- Begin with arm high, driving it down and through the target area.
- The bowling arm makes a full swing.
- Ball release position is high.
- Execute a full swing of the arms.
- Drive the back leg through to complete the action.

Variations: Use a run up and bound; increase or decrease target size; increase or decrease length; bowl underarm.

Run Up and Bowl

Objectives: To acquire and develop the skill of running up and bowling; to select and apply a range of bowling skills to effectively bowl straight and consistently hit the stump; for players to evaluate how they are bowling by listening to instructions, observing others, and analysing their own performance to improve their technique

What You'll Need: Players in groups of 4, 1 tennis ball per group, 2 sets of stumps per group

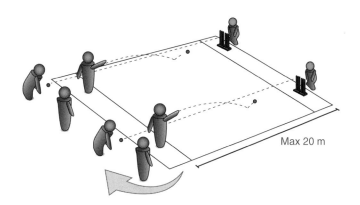

Max 20 m

Procedure: Groups of four players bowl at the stumps, as shown. One player positions behind the stumps and acts as the wicket keeper. The other players in the group stand in line on the opposite end of the playing area. The first player in line bowls the ball at the stumps, using a run up, and points are awarded for successful hits. Continue for a set number of repetitions or a set time. If necessary, the coach plays wicket keeper to judge accuracy.

Key Points
- The run up is smooth and balanced with an even stride pattern.
- The run up allows the bowler to land from the bound into tent peg 1 (back foot contact). Momentum goes down toward the target (front foot contact) with hips and shoulders in alignment to keep the action safe for tent peg 2.
- Arms swing through and legs drive through to complete the action.

Variations: Start from a base position and use a one-step method; increase or decrease the target size; increase or decrease the length of the pitch; increase the length of run up; add a batter.

Near, Middle, Far

Objectives: To acquire and develop the skill of bowling specific lengths with accuracy; to select and apply the skill of bowling accurately and at different lengths under command; to evaluate performance by observing others and listening to instructions; for players to evaluate their own technique and improve weak areas

What You'll Need: Players in any number of pairs, 1 tennis ball per pair (can use a bucket of balls if preferred), 2 sets of stumps per pair, 6 hoops (or cones) per pair

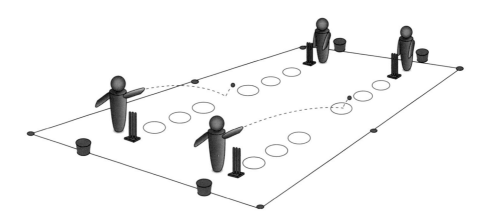

Procedure: Players position as shown and bowl to one another, trying to land the ball in the hoops (or between the cones) according to their partner's command. Partners will shout "near," "middle," or "far" prior to the ball being bowled. Continue for a set number of repetitions or a set time.

Key Points
- The run up is smooth and balanced with an even stride pattern.
- The run up allows the bowler to land from the bound into tent peg 1 (back foot contact).
- Momentum goes down toward the target (front foot contact) with hips and shoulders in alignment to keep the action safe for tent peg 2.
- Arms swing through and legs drive through to complete the action.

Variations: Start from a base position and use a one-step method; increase or decrease the target size; increase or decrease the length of the playing area; increase the length of the run up; add a batter.

Target Bowling

Objectives: To acquire and develop bowling skills to become more accurate when bowling; to select and apply bowling skills to ensure points are scored consistently; to evaluate and improve bowling by listening to instructions and observing others; for players to analyse their own execution and improve weak areas

What You'll Need: Players in groups of 6, 3 cones per group, 1 tennis ball per group, 1 set of stumps per group

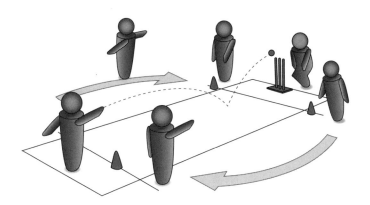

Procedure: Players take turns bowling the ball between the target coned area, attempting to hit the stumps. Once bowlers have bowled they run down to the wicket to become the wicket keeper. Once the ball is collected, the wicket keeper runs to the opposite end and passes the ball to the front player in line; she then joins the bowling queue. Points are awarded if the bowled ball lands between the cones; additional points are awarded if the ball also hits the stumps. The game continues for a set amount of repetitions or a set time.

Key Points
- The run up is smooth and balanced with an even stride pattern.
- The run up allows bowlers to land from the bound into tent peg 1 (back foot contact). Momentum goes down toward the target (front foot contact) with hips and shoulders in alignment to keep the action safe in tent peg 2.
- Arms swing through and legs drive through to complete the action.

Variations: Start from a base position and use a one-step method; increase or decrease the target size; increase or decrease the length of the playing area; increase the length of the run up; add a batter.

Coconut Shy Bowling

Objectives: To acquire and develop bowling accuracy by bowling at a large ball on the top of a stump; to select and apply skills and tactics to effectively hit the stump or ball on the stump; for players to evaluate their own technique and improve weak areas

What You'll Need: Players in groups of 4, 1 cone per group, 2 tennis balls per pair (or a bucket of balls can be used), 1 batting tee per group, 1 large ball per group

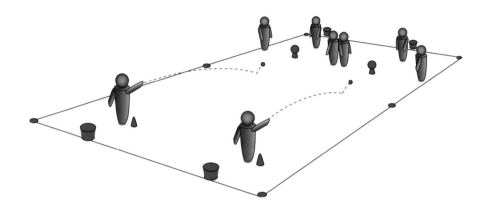

Procedure: Players take turns bowling, as shown. In place of the stump, there is a batting tee that has a large ball balanced on it. Waiting players act as fielders and wicket keepers whilst the bowler bowls. Fielders replace the ball on the stump if it is knocked off. Points can be awarded for successful hits. The game continues for a set number of repetitions or time.

Key Points
- The run up is smooth and balanced with an even stride pattern.
- The run up allows the bowler to land from the bound into tent peg 1 (back foot contact).
- Momentum goes down toward the target (front foot contact) with hips and shoulders in alignment to keep the action safe in tent peg 2.
- Arms swing through and legs drive through to complete the action.

Variations: Start from a base position and use a one-step method; increase or decrease the length of the playing area; increase the length of the run up; increase the target; add target cones; bowl underarm.

Test Bowling

Objectives: To acquire and develop the skill of bowling accurately; to apply skills and tactics to increase the amount of scoring opportunities by aiming at the base of the stumps and maximising the target area; for players to evaluate and improve their execution by listening to instructions, observing other performers, and analysing their own execution

What You'll Need: Players in pairs, 1 cone per pair, 2 tennis balls per pair (a bucket of balls can be used), 10 stumps (6, 3, 1)

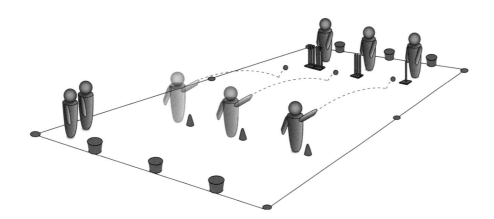

Procedure: Players work in pairs, as shown, attempting to hit the stumps while bowling. One player bowls two balls at the first target of six stumps, then bowls two balls at the next target of three stumps, and finally bowls two balls at the last target of one stump. The partner fields the balls for the partner who is bowling. Points are awarded for successful hits as follows: 1 point for hitting 6 stumps, 2 points for hitting 3 stumps, and 3 points for hitting 1 stump. After a set amount of attempts, players switch roles.

Key Points
- The run up is smooth and balanced with an even stride pattern.
- The run up allows the bowler to land from the bound into tent peg 1 (back foot contact). Momentum goes down toward the target (front foot contact) with hips and shoulders in alignment to keep the action safe in tent peg 2.
- Arms swing through and legs drive through to complete the action.

Variations: Start from a base position and use a one-step method; increase or decrease the length of the playing area; increase the length of the run up; increase the target; add target cones; bowl underarm.

Coaching Batting

The main objective of batting is to score runs. There's little point in batting if you are not going to score as many runs as you can. But you can score runs only if you are still in. A batsman is pretty useless sitting in the pavilion. In this chapter we'll discuss both how to score runs over as long a time as possible and how players should bat through an innings. Of course the two are closely related and are based on good, solid technique.

We have all experienced a plethora of coaches who teach defence, defence, defence. And you certainly need to be able to defend your wicket as a young player. However, many young players get stifled both by the heavy focus on defence and also because they are fearful to play *any* shots because the coach tells them not to get out. You have a chance to be a better coach than that. If you think back to chapter 1, the emphasis there was to ensure that your young players are having fun playing cricket. So much at the early levels is about enjoyment. And it should be. Well, the fact is that many young players enjoy attacking the ball over defending it, so the question is why should you stifle their fun? Instead, you should encourage your young players to be *positive* in their stroke play whilst understanding the longer they bat without getting out, the better they will do. Focus on how they can go out to bat and maximise their opportunities to score.

The keys to effective batting are shot selection and shot execution. In other words, batters must choose the best shot to make, and then they must effectively make that shot. Young players need to learn early on how to select their shots themselves, without the fear of a highly critical coach breathing down their necks if they make a mistake. The fact is you *want* players to make mistakes. This is how they learn. They will understand pretty fast that if they keep making the wrong choice they won't have many good games. And most youngsters want to be involved as much as possible.

By giving your players the freedom to play the shots they have learned you promote a grown-up attitude to cricket early on. Instil a self-belief in those you coach, and you'll develop players at a faster rate.

Coaching the Basics of Batting

So what should you focus on? You'll discover that some key elements are vital in helping players improve. These elements involve how to hold the bat correctly, how to stand at the crease with balance, how to swing the bat in a straight line, how to ensure the batsman lines up with the stumps, among many others. In the following sections we'll discuss some of the basics your players need to start with.

Grip

There are some unorthodox grips out there, some of them used by very accomplished batsmen. Ultimately, what matters most is that a grip is comfortable for the batsman and that it works. But there's a lot of misinformation out there about "the best way" to hold a cricket bat. For instance, you might have heard of the Vs method, in which the thumb and index finger on each hand form a V shape. A vast majority of coaches tell young players to line these Vs up, which is incorrect. What you should tell your players is that the thumbs on each hand line up to form a W shape, not overlapping Vs. The player should position the hands to form a W (figure 9.1) and then slide the bottom hand down so the thumb of the top hand just touches the wrist of the bottom hand (figure 9.2).

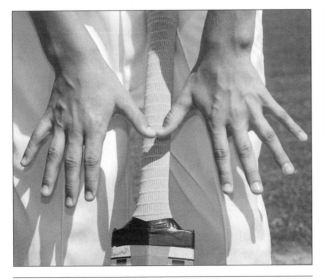

Figure 9.1   Batter's hands form a W shape on the bat.

Figure 9.2   Proper grip on the bat.

Why this small change is important is that the W grip means the back of each hand faces in almost opposite directions when the bat is held—and this is what you want, more or less. The tweaking of the top hand makes the full-extension shots, like drives, much more correct, and the batsman is less likely to hit across the line of the ball. This grip also ensures the back of the top hand doesn't slide around the back of the bat, creating top elbow line-up problems when players play forward. In addition, a batsman should not hold the bat too far down the handle to "choke" the bat; rather, only about 12 millimetres (half an inch) of the handle should show at the bottom of the bat.

Stance

The keys to a good stance are slightly relaxed knees and weight on the balls of the feet (figure 9.3). If you start your players from this position, you'll find they can move forward and backward quite easily. You are also looking for the feet to be parallel, the head level and looking at the bowler, and the chin almost touching the front shoulder in a relaxed way. The starting position of the hands is in the lap, so that the wrists feel as if they are slightly touching the pelvic bone. The bat is slightly turned in and rests against the bat foot. The turning in of the blade slightly like this, with the correct grip, starts the top hand lined up toward the bowler or mid-off, which helps with the full face of the cricket bat being presented in the straight bat shots. The starting position of the stance additionally helps the elbows of the batsman to be correctly aligned.

a   b

Figure 9.3 Proper stance for a batter: *(a)* front view and *(b)* side view.

Backswing

A good backswing of the bat occurs when the bowler is just about to deliver the ball. It helps set up the shot about to be played and thus should be a really decent backswing. It's always preferable for a young player to really pick up the bat when taking the backswing.

What you're looking for is a backswing in which the bat goes as high as the head (figure 9.4). Ideally, you want this to also be straight over off stump because this means the batsman has lifted the bat straight back. One of the easiest ways to do this is to ensure the top hand takes the bat back so that the hand is in a line above the back pocket of the trousers and lined up directly above the back foot, as shown in figure 9.5. It is the top hand that takes the bat back, while the bottom hand merely supports bat with a finger and thumb grip. Be careful the batsman doesn't simply lift the bat by cocking the wrists rather than moving the top hand in line with the pocket.

By picking up the bat correctly and with the top hand taking the bat back over off stump so the hand lines up as described, the batsman's front shoulder will be engaged correctly, too. One of the biggest problems a young batsman has is not using the front shoulder (the one facing the bowler) properly. Often, the front shoulder doesn't lean in toward the ball enough, and the backswing helps this to happen. It additionally helps to begin all the shots they play with

Figure 9.4   Correct backswing position for a batter.

Figure 9.5   Ensure the backswing is straight over off the stump by checking that the bat is in line with the back pocket.

the front shoulder first and not their feet or other part of their body. Remember that the backswing occurs before the ball is bowled, which turns the shoulder in toward the ball, which is highly desirable. Batsman should avoid "pumping" their hands up and down (like pumping water from a well) and lifting the bat rather than swinging it backward over off stump. Many players (and coaches) miss this.

Taking Guard

The idea of taking guard is so batsmen know where the off stump is. This is so they can judge what ball to play at and which ones to leave. In an ideal world, batsmen would be able to work out quickly where the ball is in relation to where they are standing. Some players like to line up the off stump with their head position just inside off stump, and some prefer the off stump to be way to the right of their eye line. Most batsmen take a leg stump, middle and leg, or middle stump guard.

> **Coaching Tip**
> Where a batsman lines up depends on what suits him or her best. But remember that most deliveries are aimed at off stump in cricket (although they often don't end up there). So think about where a batsman needs to be most of the time to play the right shot. Sometimes by simply moving the stance a little, a batsman can find it easier to get in line with the ball and be more effective.

With regards to playing the shots themselves, it makes sense with young players to initially set the ball on a tee. This tee can be set up according to the height of the ball when it reaches the batsman. You could also use coaching mats that have batting tees already built in, or you can make them yourself. It's often easier for children to learn shots from a stationary ball first so they can learn to groove their strokes. Plus a tee allows you to stand beside them and help. If you do not have something to put the ball on, you can also do a "drop feed" where you drop the ball from shoulder height on the point you want it to land so it bounces twice and the player can then hit the ball.

If you then progress to a moving ball, perhaps use "slaz" balls or tennis balls thrown underarm on the full so the batsman isn't affected by irregular bounce. Next, you could go onto underarm feeds in which the ball bounces several times to get them accustomed to a moving ball (known as "bobble" feeds). Also, don't underestimate simple feeds such as the bobble feed. Many first-class players groove their shots this way, and it can really help concentration and timing because batsmen must wait for the ball to be exactly right before they hit it.

Coaching Different Types of Shots

A batsman needs to be able to play a range of shots in a match so he can cope with different deliveries bowled. Your players' ability to decide which shot to play and then execute it is at the heart of building large team scores with the bat. So the technique of playing the most common type of shots is paramount to success. These shots will cover pitched-up deliveries and short deliveries, balls that land in line with the stumps and wider, as well as teaching attack and defence.

Drives

A batter is looking to drive a ball when attacking, and this can be off the front foot or off the back foot. The ball will be hit hard and usually results in runs. The front-foot drive is played with the weight stepping onto the front foot, and the back foot drive is played by the weight being on the back foot.

A significant feature of drive shots is that the top hand on the bat controls the shots. Try to have your players think of their top hand as the steering wheel (control) and their bottom hand as the accelerator (power). In *all* straight bat shots in which the bat remains vertical throughout the shot, it's this top hand that takes control, while the bottom hand has a minimal and light grip, sometimes with just a finger and thumb. The stronger the forearm and wrist on the top-hand side, the more control a batsman exerts over drive shots. It's worth spending time with your players to reinforce this shape and pattern.

Front-Foot Drive

The front-foot drive is played to a ball that will hit the sweet spot of the bat when stepping forward. The ball is probably landing about half to one metre (1.6 to 3.2 feet) in front of the batsman, depending on the bowler's speed. The important thing about the drive is to keep it simple. Too many coaches complicate things for young players. And with the front-foot drive, it's easy to make it seem difficult. But all you're looking to do is have the batsman "lean in" to the shot with the front shoulder to start the shot off.

This act of leaning in means the top half of the body leads the shot. We have already established that a decent backswing engages the front shoulder. So the lean-in is where the shoulder moves toward the ball first, just ahead of the feet, as shown in figure 9.6a.

After the lean-in, the front foot takes the weight of the body, and the head should be able to look over the front foot, straight down. This helps the top half to be balanced on the front foot and body position to be correct (figure 9.6b). As the knee flexes (with the foot pointing to where the ball should be hit), the hands extend through the ball (figure 9.6c) and finish with the blade of the

Coaching Tip

Many coaches say "get your foot to the pitch of the ball," but this is not technically correct. The foot doesn't get to the pitch of the ball. Rather, the batsman should aim for a decent step forward with the front foot and to maintain a stable base. This is why you don't let them take *too* large a stride—because it's harder for the top half of the body to lean forward. On a drive that goes into the leg side, the step is even shorter.

Figure 9.6   Front-foot drive.

bat pointing up to the sky (figure 9.6d). The back foot becomes simply an anchor point to keep balance, and the leg remains straight to help push the top half forward. Then the top hand is "thrown away" through the line of the ball. The arm takes the shape of a road digger, with the wrist being the bucket. The back of the hand, not the palm, should be lifted and extended to the sky.

We also want to avoid batsmen finishing their extension with their hands on their heads. This is known as "Velcro hair" and means the bat has not being driven through the ball correctly. Players with Velcro hair tend to have an incorrect top-hand grip, and the wrist collapses.

Front-Foot Defence

The front-foot defence is played to a ball that will hit the top half of the bat when stepping forward. The ball is probably landing about 2 to 3 metres (6.5 to 9.8 feet) in front of the batsman, depending on the bowler's speed. The front foot defensive drive is simply a nonextension of the front-foot drive described previously, but here the point of contact stops with the bat slightly

Figure 9.7   Front-foot defence.

ahead of the pad (figure 9.7). This is easy to play after having learned the front-foot drive because all the key points are the same. The only difference is the bat doesn't follow through or extend; it simply becomes a "dead bat."

As mentioned, the bat should ideally be slightly ahead of the front pad at contact. The reason is that if the bat and pad are tight to each other, the ball can be inside-edged from bat to pad and balloon up a catch to any close fielders. Though this is not so relevant at very young ages because of a lack of close fielders (fielding restrictions), it's important to play the shot correctly from the get-go. Also, an inside edge with the bat ahead of the pad can lead to runs down the leg side instead of the ball cannoning into the pad for no runs.

Back-Foot Drive

The back-foot drive is played to a ball that will hit the sweet spot of the bat when stepping forward. The ball is probably landing about 4 to 5 metres (13.1 to 16.4 feet) in front of the batsman, depending on the bowler's speed.

Balance is perhaps the watch word on the back-foot drive. The back foot should step back (to create more time) and across to the line of the ball. This takes the body toward the ball so the batsman can swing the bat down vertically to make contact with the ball using a straight bat and not at an angle. The step back occurs as soon as the batsman realises the ball has pitched short (closer to the bowler), and if the feet move early it gives the batsman more time to hit the ball. The concept is effectively stepping across to retake a stance with the weight slightly on the back foot. The front foot simply becomes an anchor point to stop the batsman from falling backward (figure 9.8a).

Figure 9.8   Back-foot drive.

With the weight on the back foot, the hands extend through the ball (figures 9.8 b and c) and finish with the blade of the bat pointing up to the sky (figure 9.8d). Make sure the back foot of the batsman stays sideways and doesn't point too straight down the pitch. The batsman wants to remain relatively side-on in this shot so the side that faces the bowler does all the work. It's easy for a batsman to push too hard with the bottom hand and play "across" the ball. Also, the top hand is "thrown away" through the line of the ball. The arm takes the shape of a road digger, with the wrist being the bucket. The back of the hand, not the palm, should be lifted and extended to the sky.

As with the front-foot drive, we want to avoid batsmen finishing their extension with their hands on their heads. As we mentioned earlier, this means the bat has not been driven through the ball correctly and that the top-hand grip is probably incorrect (collapsing the wrist).

Back-Foot Defence

The back-foot defence is played to a ball that will hit the top half of the bat when stepping forward. The ball is probably landing about 3 to 4 metres (9.8 to 13.1 feet) in front of the batsman, depending on the bowler's speed. The back-foot defence is simply a nonextension of the back-foot drive described previously, but here the point of contact stops with the bat slightly ahead of the pad (figure 9.9). This is easy to play after having learned the back-foot drive because all the key points are the same. The only difference is the bat doesn't follow through or extend but simply becomes a dead bat.

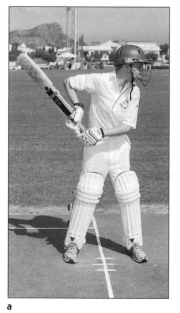

a   b   c

Figure 9.9   Back-foot defence.

Square of the Wicket Shots

Now let's move on to some square of the wicket shots, such as the cut and pull shot. With the drives, the top hand is very dominant, but with the squarer shots, it is the *bottom* hand that dictates the shot. If your players understand this, they'll often find it easier to get into the correct position and hit the ball far better.

It's also important, to maximise power, that these shots are played at arm's length with the bottom hand. You'll find that on short-pitched deliveries, in which the batsman has time and room to swing the bat horizontally, the free swing of the blade makes contact somewhere near the middle of the bat. The cut shot is hit into the off side, whereas the pull shot is played into the leg side.

Square Cut

The square cut is played to a ball that will hit the sweet spot of the bat when stepping back and across toward the offside. The ball is probably landing about 4 to 5 metres (13.1 to 16.4 feet) in front of the batsman, depending on the bowler's speed, and wide enough to free up the arms. Like the back-foot drive, this is an attacking shot but is played away from the body.

The square cut requires a batsman to make a larger, deeper step across the stumps (figure 9.10a). The supporting leg (the front leg in this case) is left slightly open so the batsman can maintain balance when swinging the bat. The feeling of the square cut is more like chopping down a tree, which should give you an idea of the horizontal movement of the plane of the bat.

The weight is supported on the back leg, and the knee flexes as the shoulders turn into the shot and the bat hits through the line of the ball (figure 9.10 b and c). The aim is to hit the ball just ahead of cover point, or just behind, depending on the speed of the bowler, width of the ball, and how much the ball bounces. Also, the hands are "thrown" through the ball with a full arm extension. The bottom hand controls the blade of the bat and rolls over the ball to help keep the ball down. Make sure body weight is over the back leg and moving into the ball, not away from it. The top of the shot is similar to that of the pull shot (described next) in that they are both bottom-hand controlled and across-the-line shots. The finishing point for the square cut is the batsman's head looking over the back shoulder (figure 9.10d).

Pull Shot

The shot is played to a ball that will hit the sweet spot of the bat when stepping back and hitting across the line. The ball is probably landing about 4 to 5 metres (13.1 to 16.4 feet) in front of the batsman, depending on the bowler's speed, and short enough to free up the arms. This is an attacking shot but with the connection point way in front of the body. The pull shot is a great shot to master for any young cricketer because it helps with their fear of being hit by a ball. If a batsman can easily pull cricket balls for four, it gives great confidence.

Figure 9.10 Square cut.

Classically, the pull shot is taught by stepping back with the back leg first, then opening up the front leg by stepping toward the square-leg umpire so the batsman is totally facing the bowler when hitting the ball. But there is a better way to play this shot without the necessity for the second step, which means a faster movement and an easier position to pull from. Also, 99 per-cent of pull shots are played more from a back-foot drive base position. The batsman should step straight back toward the stumps to create some space to play this shot (figure 9.11a). The back foot points toward mid-off for this step rather than sideways. This is what helps the hip to open out (rather than the need to step to square leg next). The front foot comes onto the ball of the

Figure 9.11 Pull shot.

foot and helps push slightly backward at the same time. This gives a balanced stance to pull from, with the weight on the back leg but the top half leaning slightly in toward the ball.

The batsman swings the hands away from the body and through the ball with maximum extension, so that the contact on the bat is made at full arm's length (figure 9.11 b and c). As with the cut shot, the feeling of the pull shot is more like chopping down a tree. Sometimes the bat swings through and the batsman pivots a little bit on the back foot, like a hammer thrower. World-class players, who have less time to react against the fast bowling at this level, use the pivot pull concept to ensure and maintain a smooth shot and balance throughout. This movement shortens the time it takes to move the feet and reduces the need for large base movements that can take time and hurry the actual shot. The top of the shot is similar to the square cut's in that they are both bottom-hand controlled and across-the-line shots. The finishing point on both is the batsman's head looking over the back shoulder (figure 9.11d).

Creative Shots

There are other shots that require the batter to be a bit more creative. This can mean hitting the ball in the air or using the speed of the ball to deflect the ball into certain areas of the outfield. Creative shots are very useful for helping a team score more runs and might also help shift the game toward the batting side if the fielding side is threatening to dominate. The two most common creative shots are hitting the ball over the top of the infield and glancing the ball into gaps off the batsman's legs, where there are fewer fielders.

Leg Glance

The leg glance is played from the back-foot or the front-foot position similar to the back-foot or front-foot defence. The setup is the same as for those deliveries except that on the point of contact the blade of the bat is turned so the ball is deflected into the leg side (see figure 9.12 for an example of a front-foot leg glance and figure 9.13 for an example of a back-foot leg glance). You might find that a batsman tries to hit this ball to leg by hitting across the line of the ball, but it should be a full-face shot and a turn of the top hand into the leg side to change the angle of the blade. The blade of the bat is kept straight by the elbow of the front arm, which is kept high. This allows the face of the bat to make a clean contact as the wrist turns it into the leg side. Again, like the straight-bat shots, the top hand controls the stroke, and the bottom hand simply helps turn the blade over.

The glance is a simple shot to play if the base positions are adhered to. This is because the only

Coaching Tip

The importance in playing this shot well is to maintain the *shape of the shot* so it looks like any forward or backward defensive shot would look. Good form equals good execution of the shot.

Figure 9.12 Front-foot leg glance.

thing the batsman now thinks about is to effectively "nudge" the ball behind square on the leg side. Effectively, once in position, an easy turn of the bat blade is all that's required to complete the shot. At junior level, many deliveries get bowled by mistake down the leg side or at leg stump. This means there are plenty of opportunities for young batters to play this shot—and it can be amazingly effective.

Figure 9.13   Back-foot leg glance.

Hitting Over the Top

Hitting the ball intentionally into the air and over fielders is an exhilarating shot, yet it can be fraught with dangers. The main danger is not making a clean connection with the ball and simply dragging it, lofting it, or skewing it off the edge of the bat and straight to a fielder. Although hitting over the top is associated with how to play shots against spin or slow bowlers, it can also be very effective against faster bowlers. As with all shots, it is the base and shape of the shot that matter when trying to create proper execution.

The length of ball for a lofted shot depends on the speed of the bowler and whether the batsman is coming down the pitch to reach the ball. With a slow bowler, tossing the ball invitingly in the air, the batsman might decide to leave his crease and meet the ball, thus effectively changing its length to something easier to hit. It is this advancing, or "coming down the pitch" that can be done in a couple of different ways.

The first is almost like a crow hop in fielding, in which the front foot and then the back foot advance the batsman toward the ball (figure 9.14). The

Figure 9.14 Batter advancing using the crow hop.

back foot goes behind the front foot, as shown in figure 9.14b, and helps push forward so the final step is effectively like playing a normal front-foot drive but from further down the pitch, as shown in figure 9.14c. This feels like a gallop or a side to side "bounce" and creates momentum into the shot.

The second method is almost like walking down the pitch, literally, with the back foot passing the front foot in front of the body and not behind (figure 9.15). This is done so the batsman can be relaxed and maintain a level eye movement without bouncing up and down.

a

b

c

d

Figure 9.15 Batter advancing by walking down the pitch.

Once at the position the batsman wishes to loft the ball from, make sure he or she hits the ball a little earlier so the bat comes underneath the ball and takes it aerially (figures 9.16a and b). The ending of the shot is a full follow-through and hand extension to make certain all the power goes into the ball and not across it (figure 9.16c). Of course, the batsman can hit over the top by staying in the crease and hitting through the line of the ball. Often a good length ball, that would require a forward defensive shot, can be lofted back over the bowler's head. Sometimes it can be as simple as just hitting the ball earlier, thus getting a drive upward instead of downward.

Figure 9.16   Hitting over the top.

Hitting over the top isn't just reserved for straight shots. They can be lifted from square cuts, pull shots, glances, and sweep shots. The principle is the same—hit early and stay in the shot. Note, however, that if a batsman is hitting into the air, it's important to ensure they go completely through with any shot. It's better to hit the ball hard than to hit it half-heartedly and risk giving a catch. In other words, the batsman should fully commit to the stroke instead of bailing out halfway through. The importance here of a stable base cannot be overstated. It's far easier to hit cleanly with a steady head and strong base than to swing wildly with the head in the clouds. However, if batsmen feel they are *not* going to make the distance when coming down the pitch, they can always simply block the ball. There's no shame in changing their minds—just as long as they are not caught between two ideas. So the message to give your batsmen is this: Commit to what you plan to do unless it is obvious you can't do it; then just block the ball. If you are attacking and committed, go right through without stopping the shot halfway. This is what usually happens to young players caught in two minds. They end up doing neither.

Coaching Running Between the Wickets

However well your young charges bat, chances are good they will be the square root of pretty awful at running between the wickets. Judging when to run is possibly the greatest challenge for any young batsman. And this has nothing to do with how good a player they are, either.

Judging how far the ball has travelled, how fast they can run, whether a fielder can make a stop and throw it, whether their partner can run, and not wanting to be run out—these are all factors in running between the wickets. These decisions are increased in difficulty by inexperience and age. Plus, batsmen often fail to think about the wider picture of running with a partner at the other end who must also make his or her ground safely.

Spend time on drills in which your batsmen practice calling and running in various scenarios with fielders. In just two simple practice sessions, your club side could make dramatic improvements in both speed between the wickets and judgement of runs. This could lead to an extra 30 or 40 runs per innings in an afternoon match. These sessions can be run by coaches or captains and don't require much equipment beyond normal cricket stuff. After warming up, this is what you do:

Coaching Tip

There are three calls when running between the wickets: yes, no, or wait. Yes is a definite run. No is definitely not. Wait is a maybe but will be followed quickly by a yes or no. These calls are made by the batsman if the ball goes in front of the batting stumps, and by the non-striker if the ball goes behind the batting stumps. The reason is that the person running to the likely "danger end" should make the call.

Practice Session 1: Improving Technique

In recent times coaches have learned the importance of technique on running speed. Your first practice session will focus on taking some important points from the world of sprinting and translating them to cricket.

Setting Off

"Always run the first run hard" is an adage that remains true. The first few steps should get a runner to top speed as soon as possible, as either striker or nonstriker. The most important points to remember can be seen in figure 9.17. The runner keeps the head down and stays low, like a sprinter coming out of the blocks, and holds the bat across the body while focusing on pumping the arms. This should lead to short, fast steps as the runner focuses on going from almost stationary to top speed. The foot is behind the centre of gravity, the angle of the shin acute. This maximises the force the leg muscles can produce. The feel at this stage should be almost overbalancing.

Figure 9.17   Setting off.

Hitting Your Stride

About a third of the way down the pitch, the runner starts to take longer strides and the head comes up. This is important for speed, plus the runner wants to remain aware of where the ball is. The key element is arm speed. The faster the runner pumps his arms with the bat across his body, the faster his legs will go. As shown in figure 9.18, the runner is still leaning forward, letting momentum carry him, but he is no longer accelerating. This is the best position to be in to move to the next phase of slowing and turning for another run.

Figure 9.18   Hitting your stride.

Coaching Tip

To practice hitting your stride, take it in turns to run singles focusing on the correct technique of accelerating, hitting your stride, and sliding the bat in. Once you are comfortable running singles alone, make it a race between two teams to add pressure. The focus should remain on proper technique at this point.

An exception to this technique might be when running a tight run in a match. Here runners know where the ball is already, and their only aim is to make it to the other end as fast as possible with no thought of turning. Instead of hitting a stride, they can continue to accelerate with head down, only slowing slightly to slide the bat in.

Decelerate, Turn, and Go

If not running a quick single, the runner is usually looking for a second run. This makes the speed of the turn very important. According to recent coaching advice from the ECB, the fastest way to turn includes the following elements, which you can share with your players:

- Wait to the last moment in the approach to the crease to slow down. As you reach the crease, slow yourself by sinking your hips and sitting back slightly (figure 9.19a).
- Get as low as possible to the ground, using one hand to slide the bat over the line in the classic sideways position (figure 9.19b).
- Push off hard with the leg closest to the crease (figure 9.19c).
- Accelerate into the run, staying low, using the setting-off technique (described earlier).

To coach the decelerate, turn, and go, use a long stick that players must slide under to learn how to stay low in the turn. Hold it at arm's length like a limbo bar and have runners keep low as they reach beneath it and slide and then

Figure 9.19 Decelerate, turn, and go.

touch their bat into the crease. Or place the stick across two cones a metre (3.2 feet) from the crease line at about chest or waist height. The objective is for the runner to avoid touching that bar. Again, start with learning the technique, and then add a competitive element to increase the pressure.

You can see dramatic technical improvements in one session. However, running technique needs work to be developed further. There's no need to turn everyone into a sprinter, but you should schedule regular sessions that work on the technique of running between the wickets if you want to keep your team switched on.

Practice Session 2: Awareness

The second practice session is less about technique and more about judging a run more accurately. So there's a lot more fun cricket stuff happening during this practice. Start the session with a discussion between players on best practice when running. This is up to the players to decide but could include the following:

- Early calls of yes, no, or wait. Nothing else.
- Backing up from the nonstriker.
- Talking about weak fielders to put pressure on.
- Identifying which fielders are weak to the right- or left-hand side and running harder if the ball goes to the weak side.

The way to do this might be to use two sets of stumps and have balls rolled to fielders from those stumps to fielders, so batsmen can practice calling correctly. Better still, and as a follow-up to that, hit balls into a fielding circle to create both exciting fielding practice as well as running between the wickets practice. This leads to developing judgement for batsmen regarding when to run, what to call, and how to work out distances given their running speed.

Batting Drills

You can use the following drills along with the key points we have already discussed. Modify the drills to suit your needs with your team.

For each drill you'll find the objectives of the drill, the equipment needed, the organization and setup, instructions on how to run the drill, the technique you are looking for, and ways to make the drill either easier or harder, depending on the age and skill level of your players. Also review Appendix C: 15 Game-Based Drills on page 175.

Line Batting

Objectives: To acquire and develop decision-making skills to improve shot selection; to select and apply skills to use the correct shot to the line and length of the ball received; to evaluate performance by observing others and listening to and following instructions

What You'll Need: Players in groups of 7, 4 cones per group, 6 tennis balls per group, 1 set of stumps per group; 1 bat per player

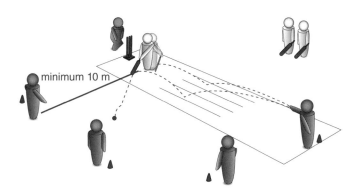

minimum 10 m

Procedure: Groups of seven players are organised as shown. The coach serves the ball into the ground toward the batter. The feed should be varied, with balls hit into each of the three channels between the cones. Balls landing in the off-side channel should be hit on the off side, balls pitching in line should be hit straight, and leg-side channel deliveries should be hit on the leg side. Points can be awarded for correct shots to appropriate deliveries. The fielders positioned between the cones field the balls and throw them back to the coach. Each player has a set number of repetitions. The drill continues for a set time or until all players have had a go.

Key Points
- When batting, adopt a balanced stance with head level and include bat tap, backswing, and a step forward or back.
- Batter watches the ball and makes a decision on the direction to hit the ball.
- Batter takes a comfortable stride, and shoulders rotate vertically to begin downswing.
- Maintain shape with bat and arms.
- Batter swings the bat through the line of the ball to complete the follow-through.

Variations: Hit the ball off a batting tee; use bobble serves; use overarm throws; use different balls; increase or decrease serving distance; fielders can catch the ball; increase or decrease the size or distance of the channels.

Length Batting

Objectives: To acquire and develop decision-making skills to improve shot selection; to select and apply skills to use the correct shot to the line and length of the ball received; to evaluate performance by observing others and listening to and following instructions

What You'll Need: Players in groups of 5, 4 cones per group, 6 tennis balls per group (or a bucket of balls can be used), 1 set of stumps per group, 1 bat per group

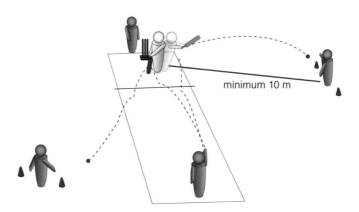

minimum 10 m

Procedure: Groups of five players are organised as shown. The bowler serves the ball into the ground toward the batter. The feed should be varied, with balls bouncing in front of or behind the line marked. Balls landing in front of the line should be hit on the front foot; balls landing behind the line should be hit off the back foot. Points can be awarded for correct shots to appropriate deliveries. The batter hits balls into each of the three channels between the cones, and fielders positioned between the cones field the balls and throw them back to the bowler. Each player has a set number of repetitions. The drill continues for a set time or until all players have had a go.

Key Points
- When batting, adopt a balanced stance with head level and include bat tap, backswing, and a step forward or back.
- Batter watches the ball and makes a decision on the direction to hit the ball.
- Batter takes a comfortable stride, and shoulders rotate vertically to begin downswing.
- Maintain shape with bat and arms.
- Batter swings the bat through the line of the ball to complete the follow-through.

Variations: Hit the ball off a batting tee; use bobble serves; use overarm throws; use different balls; increase or decrease serving distance; fielders can catch the ball; increase or decrease the size or distance of the channels.

Back-Foot Manipulation

Objectives: To acquire and develop the skill of manipulating the ball off the back foot; to select and apply back-foot shots according to the line of the delivery; to evaluate performance by observing others and listening to and following instructions; to learn to self-analyse to identify which technical and tactical areas to improve

What You'll Need: Players in groups of 4, 13 cones per group, 6 tennis balls per group (or a bucket of balls can be used), 1 set of stumps per group, 1 bat per group

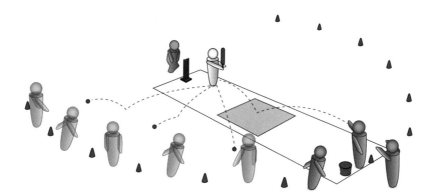

Procedure: Groups are organised as shown. The coach or teacher serves the ball so it lands short of a length with one bounce. The fielder takes a position between a predetermined set of cones, and the batter attempts to hit the ball to that coned area. Points can be awarded for successful attempts. All players should have a set amount of goes each.

Key Points
- When batting, adopt a balanced stance with head level and include bat tap, backswing, and step back.
- Batter watches the ball and makes a decision on the direction to hit the ball.
- Batter takes a comfortable stride; shoulders rotate vertically to begin downswing.
- Maintain shape with bat and arms.
- Batter swings the bat through the line of the ball to complete the follow-through.

Variations: Hit the ball off a batting tee; use bobble serves; use overarm throws; use different balls; use a bowling machine; use full batting equipment; increase or decrease serving distance; increase or decrease the size or distance of the area between the cones.

Front-Foot Manipulation

Objectives: To acquire and develop the skill of manipulating the ball off the front foot; to select and apply front-foot shots according to the line of the delivery; to evaluate performance by observing others and listening to and following instructions; to use self-analysis to identify which technical and tactical areas need improvement

What You'll Need: Players in groups of 4, 13 cones per group, 6 tennis balls per group (or a bucket of balls can be used), 1 set of stumps per group, 1 bat per group

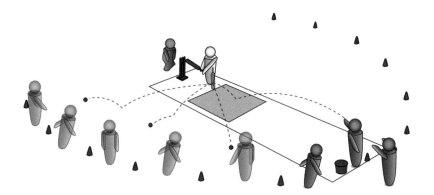

Procedure: Groups are organised as shown. The coach or teacher serves the ball so it lands on a full length. The fielder positions between a predetermined set of cones, and the batter attempts to hit the ball to that coned area. Points can be awarded for successful attempts. All players should have a set amount of goes each.

Key Points
- When batting, adopt a balanced stance with head level and include bat tap, backswing, and a step forward.
- Watch the ball and decide on the direction to hit.
- Batter takes a comfortable stride; shoulders rotate vertically to begin downswing.
- Maintain shape with bat and arms.
- Batter swings the bat through the line of the ball to complete the follow-through.

Variations: Hit the ball off a batting tee; use bobble serves; use overarm throws; use different balls; increase or decrease serving distance; increase or decrease the size or distance of the coned areas.

Off Drive

Objectives: To acquire and develop the skill of driving the ball on the off side; to select and apply drives on the off side according to the line of the delivery; to evaluate performance by observing others and listening to and following instructions; to use self-analysis to identify which technical and tactical areas to work on

What You'll Need: Players in groups of 8, 5 cones per group, 6 tennis balls per group, 1 set of stumps per group, 1 bat per group

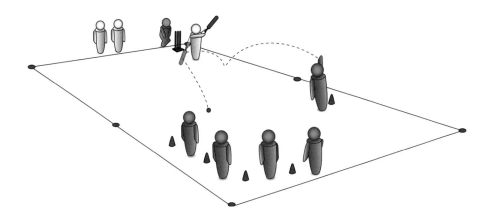

Procedure: Players are organised as shown; groups are broken down into two teams of four. The batting team stands behind the striking batsman in a safe area. Fielders line up 1 metre (3.2 feet) behind the coned area and must not encroach. The coach or teacher serves the ball so it lands as a half-volley on the off side. Batter attempts to hit the ball toward the coned area to score points, which are given for hitting between the cones. All players should have a set amount of goes each.

Key Points
- When batting, adopt a balanced stance with head level and include bat tap, backswing, and a step forward or back.
- Watch the ball and decide on the direction to hit.
- Batter takes a comfortable stride; shoulders rotate vertically to begin downswing.
- Maintain shape with bat and arms.
- Bat swings through the line of the ball to complete the follow-through.

Variations: Hit the ball off a batting tee; use bobble serves; use overarm throws; use different balls; increase or decrease serving distance; increase or decrease the size of the coned areas.

Back-Foot Forcing

Objectives: To acquire and develop the skill of attacking straight bat shots off the back foot; to select and apply the skill according to line and length of the direction of the ball; to evaluate performance by observing others and by listening to and following instructions

What You'll Need: Players in groups of 8, 5 cones per group, 6 tennis balls per group, 1 set of stumps per group, 1 bat per group

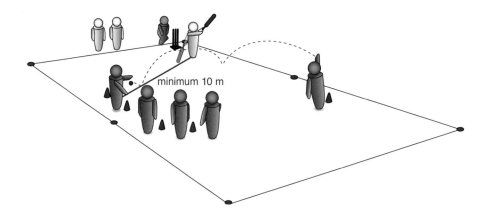

minimum 10 m

Procedure: Players are organised as shown; break groups down into two teams of four. The batting team stands behind the striking batsman in a safe area. Fielders line up 1 metre (3.2 feet) behind the coned area and must not encroach. The coach or teacher serves the ball with one bounce to the batter. The batter makes a decision to play the ball off the back foot into the coned area. Points can be awarded for successful execution of the shot. Players rotate and have equal goes within the time allocated.

Key Points
- When batting, adopt a balanced stance with head level and include bat tap, backswing, and a step forward or back.
- Watch the ball and decide on the direction to hit.
- Batter takes a comfortable stride; shoulders rotate vertically to begin downswing.
- Maintain shape with bat and arms.
- The bat swings through the line of the ball to complete the follow-through.

Variations: Hit the ball off a batting tee; use bobble serves; use overarm throws; use different balls; increase or decrease serving distance; increase or decrease the size or distance of the coned areas.

Play Straight

Objectives: To acquire and develop straight bat shot and fielding skills under pressure; to select and apply skills and tactics to increase or decrease scoring opportunities; for players to evaluate and improve execution by listening to and following instructions, by observing others perform, and by analysing their own execution to identify areas to improve

What You'll Need: Players in groups of 12, 1 tennis ball per group, 2 sets of stumps per group, 2 bats

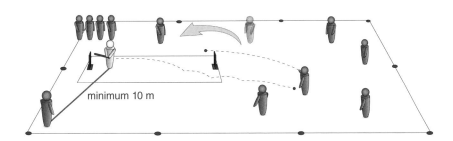

minimum 10 m

Procedure: A group of players is broken into two teams of six, as shown. For the batting team, two batters are at the stumps, one batter stands near one of the stumps waiting for a turn at bat, and the rest of the players line up behind the stumps, a safe distance away. For the fielding team, players are dispersed throughout the playing area. To begin, the coach or teacher drops the ball from arm's length, and the batter strikes the ball on the bounce (batter will be out if he fails to hit the ball beyond the far stumps). Batters run to the far stumps and back if the ball goes past the far set of stumps. Fielders attempt to field the ball; if the ball is caught, it doesn't count as an out. Once the ball is fielded, the fielder attempts to run the batter out by throwing the ball at the stumps. A ball hit past the fielders is worth 4 runs. Balls hit in this fashion but along the floor are awarded 6 points. The practice continues for a set amount of time per innings, allowing dismissed batters to come back in, or until the innings is complete.

Key Points
- When batting, adopt a balanced stance with head level and include bat tap, backswing, and a step forward or back.
- Watch the ball and decide on the direction to hit.
- Batter takes a comfortable stride; shoulders rotate vertically to begin downswing.
- Maintain shape with bat and arms.
- The bat swings through the line of the ball to complete the follow-through.

Variations: Hit the ball off a batting tee; use bobble serves; use overarm throws; use different balls; fielders can catch the ball resulting in an out; increase or decrease the size of the area the batsman hits to.

Square Cut

Objectives: To acquire and develop the skill of playing the square cut; to select and apply the square cut according to the line and length of the delivery; to evaluate performance by observing others and listening to and following instructions and by using self-analysis to identify which technical and tactical areas to improve

What You'll Need: Players in groups of 8, 5 cones per group, 6 tennis balls per group, 1 set of stumps per group, 1 bat per group

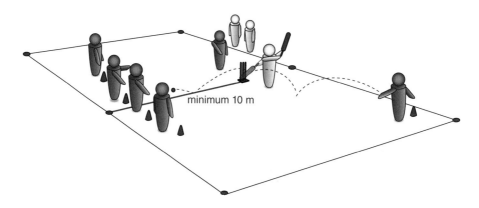

minimum 10 m

Procedure: Players organise as shown; break groups down into two teams of four. For the batting team, one player is at bat, one player waits near the stumps for a turn at bat, and the remaining two players wait behind the batting team's cone, a safe distance away. For the fielding team, players position between cones. The coach or teacher serves a ball short and wide of off stump to the batter. Fielders attempt to catch the batter out. Players rotate after a set number of goes or after a set time.

Key Points
- When batting, adopt a balanced stance with head level and include bat tap, backswing, and step back and across
- Watch the ball and decide on the direction to hit.
- Weight is established on back leg.
- Shoulders rotate horizontally to off side.
- Hit high to low with a natural follow-through.

Variations: Use bobble serves; use overarm throws; use different balls; increase or decrease serving distance; increase or decrease the size or distance of the coned areas.

Lofted Drive

Objectives: To acquire and develop the skill of playing the lofted drive; to select and apply lofted drives according to the line and length of the delivery; to evaluate performance by observing others and listening to and following instructions; to use self-analysis to identify which technical and tactical areas need improvement

What You'll Need: Players in groups of 12, 6 cones per group, 6 tennis balls per group, 1 set of stumps per group, 1 bat per group

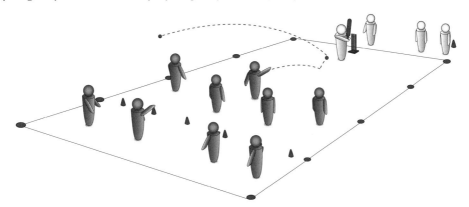

Procedure: Players organise as shown; break groups down into a fielding team of eight and a batting team of four. For the batting team, one player is at bat, one player waits near the stumps for a turn at bat, and the remaining two players wait behind the batting team's cone, a safe distance away. Cones are positioned 30 metres (98 feet) away from the batter. One fielding group of four positions in the middle area, and the other fielding group of four positions in the back area, as shown. Fielders must not encroach. The coach serves the ball so it lands on a length. The batter attempts to hit the ball in the air toward the coned area. Points can be awarded for successful attempts that reach the coned area. All players should have a set amount of goes each.

Key Points
- When batting, adopt a balanced stance with head level and include bat tap, backswing, and a step forward or back.
- Watch the ball and decide on the direction to hit.
- Batter takes a comfortable stride; shoulders rotate vertically to begin downswing.
- Maintain shape with bat and arms.
- The bat swings through the line of the ball to complete the follow-through.
- Hit the ball slightly early to allow the ball to be lofted.
- Maintain balance with weight slightly behind the ball.

Variations: Hit the ball off a batting tee; use bobble serves; use overarm throws; use different balls; increase or decrease the serving distance; fielders can catch the ball; increase or decrease the length the cones are positioned from the batter.

On Drive

Objectives: To acquire and develop the skill of driving the ball on the off side; to select and apply drives on the off side according to the line of the delivery; to evaluate performance by observing others and listening to and following instructions; to use self-analysis to identify technical and tactical areas that need improvement

What You'll Need: Players in groups of 8, 6 cones per group, 6 tennis balls per group, 1 set of stumps per group, 1 bat per group

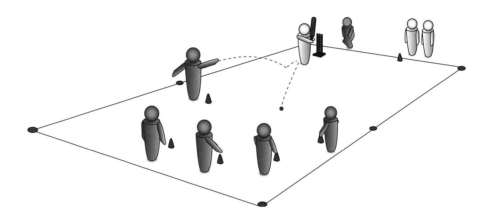

Procedure: Players are organised as shown; break groups down into two teams of four. The batting team stands behind the striking batsman in a safe area. Fielders position 1 metre (3.2 feet) behind the coned area and must not encroach. The coach serves the ball so it lands as a half-volley on the on side. The batter attempts to hit the ball toward the coned area to score points. All players should have a set amount of goes each.

Key Points
- When batting, adopt a balanced stance with head level and include bat tap, backswing, and a step forward or back.
- Watch the ball and decide on the direction to hit.
- Batter takes a comfortable stride; shoulders rotate vertically to begin downswing.
- Maintain shape with bat and arms.
- The bat swings through the line of the ball to complete the follow-through.

Variations: Hit the ball off a batting tee; use bobble serves; use overarm throws; use different balls; increase or decrease serving distance; fielders can catch the ball; increase or decrease the area between the cones.

Back-Foot Defensive

Objectives: To acquire and develop the skill of playing the back defence; to select and apply the back defence according to the line of the delivery; to evaluate performance by observing others and listening to and following instructions; to use self-analysis to identify which technical and tactical areas to work on

What You'll Need: Players in groups of 6, 1 cone per group, 6 tennis balls per group, 1 set of stumps per group, 1 bat per group

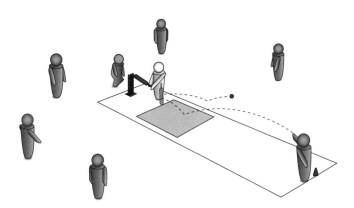

Procedure: Players are organised as shown. The coach or teacher serves a ball on back of a good length to the batter. Fielders attempt to catch the batter out. Players rotate after a set number of goes or after a set time, so they get to field in every position. Individual points could be scored for not being caught or for hitting the ball into an area directed by the coach.

Key Points
- When batting, adopt a balanced stance with head level and include bat tap, backswing, and a step forward or back.
- Watch the ball and decide on the direction to hit.
- Batter takes a comfortable stride, and shoulders rotate vertically to begin the downswing.
- Maintain shape with bat and arms.
- The bat swings through the line of the ball to complete the follow-through.

Variations: Use bobble serves; use overarm throws; use different balls; increase or decrease the distance of the fielders' positions.

Front-Foot Defensive

Objectives: To acquire and develop the skill of playing the forward defence; to select and apply the forward defence according to the line and length of the delivery; to evaluate performance by observing others and listening to and following instructions; to use self-analysis to identify which technical and tactical areas to work on

What You'll Need: Players in groups of 6, 1 cone per group, 6 tennis balls per group, 1 set of stumps per group, 1 bat per group

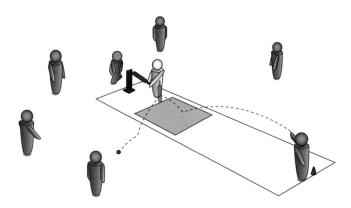

Procedure: Players are organised as shown. The coach serves a ball on a good length to the batter. Fielders attempt to catch the batter out. Players rotate after a set number of goes or after a set time, so they get to field in every position. Points can be scored for not being caught or for hitting the ball into an area directed by the coach.

Key Points
- When batting, adopt a balanced stance with head level and include bat tap, backswing, and a step forward.
- Watch the ball and decide on the direction to hit.
- Batter takes a comfortable stride; shoulders rotate vertically to begin downswing.
- Maintain shape with bat and arms.
- The bat swings through the line of the ball to complete the follow-through.

Variations: Use bobble serves and spin serves; use overarm throws; use different balls; increase or decrease serving distance; increase or decrease the distance of the fielders' positions.

Coaching on Match Day

Coaching on match day is exhausting for coaches and players alike but is nearly always exciting. This is when adrenaline kicks in and young players consequently make more mistakes. If you're coaching a very young team, you might know already how excited your players get on match day. How you control this excitement dictates how well your team plays. You don't want to suppress their excitement, but you do want to channel it.

The same goes for parents. Some parents are quite anxious about their children's cricket. Some become agitated, which is sometimes understandable. It's your duty to provide clear goals to both players and parents about expectations. Many parents will want to be around their children as much as they can, and however well meaning they are, you must decide if this is what you want as a coach. Will parents be disruptive toward your ability to take charge? Are they likely to get in the way when it comes to trying to rally the players into a cohesive unit? These are just two of your match-day challenges.

Sometimes parents want to coach their own children, or at least to advise them on match days, often sitting on the sidelines shouting to their kids. Others simply yell out general encouragement to the team. You have to decide how much of this is acceptable. This is a difficult area to address because you don't want to alienate parents. But you also don't want them to undermine you as coach or to distract your team. As you might expect, dealing with parents on match day (and other days) requires strong communication skills on your part.

Begin by laying down some ground rules for match days for both players and parents to adhere to. Such rules are often best communicated through writing so that everyone can refer to them and is clear on expectations ahead of time. Be sure to cover match-day issues well before the games themselves. The preseason is the best time for this, or when you first announce squads.

Assuming all parents are "onside" with the match-day rules, let's get to your role as a coach. First, always remember that whatever you have spent time practicing in nets players might not easily be able to re-create in the middle. Some players are simply unable to perform under pressure as they do in nets or practice. Others get far too nervous with the pressure of friends or family watching. Fear of failure for young players can be overwhelming, so help them out by reminding them that cricket is not life or death, just fun.

Before the Match

As a coach it's your duty to encourage your players to go out and do the best they can as a team. Some players will be interested primarily in how they do as individuals, but this is perfectly natural. Your role is to try and help all players identify with the team and realise that what they do affects everyone else. If you can build team spirit, you'll find that a group of players with average talent can sometimes achieve above-average results.

As good a place to start as any is punctuality. Time keeping is a vital part of respect and discipline in a player's career, so instil in your players how important it is to be on time. Of course this includes you. It's probably best to get to the grounds nice and early so you can check on conditions such as the state of the pitch and the weather. If you're playing away, you'll also need to arrive early, so set an example and expect others to follow.

If the weather is poor and the match is clearly unplayable, try to contact players, parents, or opposition in enough time to save them from travelling. If it's a great day, you'll want to arrive early to ensure lines are marked out, the pitch prepared, and so on. Have you remembered to notify umpires and scorers, if necessary? Do you have enough cricket balls for the match? Do all your players have equipment, or do you need to supply some? These are obvious things to tend to but can be overlooked.

Once your players begin to arrive, you'll want to prepare them for the match, including warming up, stretching, and a fielding routine to get them tuned into the day. Do this at least 30 minutes before the match to send the message to the opposition that your team is organised and ready to play. It can be disarming to see a team all suited up and methodically drilling well ahead of game time.

Another prematch task at some levels is to write up the team sheet or at least discuss your team to let the opposing coach know who is going to play. Depending on how many kids you have on your team, there might be some tough decisions on whom to leave out and whom to play. The key is to keep everyone involved over the course of a season. Balance playing time so all players get to play a somewhat even share. Consider explaining this policy at the beginning of the season to alleviate player anxiety and take the pressure off yourself as well.

Those you leave off the team for a match should be made to feel part of the squad and useful. Perhaps they can help you in certain activities. If your team is truly a squad of players, there should be an element of everyone "mucking in." For example, you can make non-players "active 12th men" where they assist with drinks, organisation on the day, and provide general support for the rest of the players.

Once you have selected the day's team, you'll have to choose a batting order, or if the team is an older one, you might let your captain choose the order under your guidance. Your role is to be there to guide and facilitate as much as possible. If you're unsure about the best batting order, you might sit players down and ask what number they would like to bat. Be prepared for most of them to say in the top four, but also watch for shy or quiet players who won't speak up for themselves. You might have to speak up for them at first.

During the Match

This is when a coach's job can be frustrating. Not everything you have planned will turn out the way you hoped. You might as well expect the unexpected. Seen the right way, surprises are truly part of the fun in being a coach. All your work and effort is being put to the test, and it's fun to see how everything plays out. There's always the question: How much should you intervene as coach, and how much should you just let things evolve? This can be a tricky balance, but a good rule of thumb is the younger the players, the more the guidance. Be supportive enough that players know you're there to help them, but don't be so overbearing that they feel smothered. Do remind your young cricketers of the key points they have been practicing. This will give them the confidence to go out in a competitive environment and put them into play.

Your main ally on the field is your captain. He or she is the focus of helping you implement many of the basics you have been working toward as a team. But this player will need a great deal of encouragement because he or she shouldn't feel overawed with the responsibility of having on-field duties. Help your captain out with things like field placing. If you have an idea of what sort of field placing each bowler should bowl to, you can help instil that into the bowlers themselves. It will significantly help out your captain if your squad's bowlers know what they are doing with fielders. Bowling changes should also be left to your captain, but you can help here. Should a spinner be bowling early or later in a match? What end do they bowl from? Is there a breeze or slope that can assist certain types of bowler (swing or spin)? These are some of the questions that contribute to creating an understanding of who bowls when and from where. It does completely depend on what level of player and age group you are working with, too. Very young players or beginners are simply not likely to have enough knowledge of cricket to make independent decisions without your guidance. Older, senior players with a good deal of cricket under their belts ought to be encouraged to make those tough choices themselves.

Much of what you have practiced—fielding drills, concentration, learning to back each other up in the field, watching the ball at all times, expecting the ball, and so on—you will want to re-enforce for your team. You can encourage that from the side and help your captain and players by getting the team to shout out supportive words and phrases when players execute well or do something excellent. Vocal support also helps players know what to do at a particular time.

Your players on the field should try to be vocal themselves, getting involved as much as possible and not waiting for something to happen. Indeed, by keeping spirits high in the field, a fielding team can often start to overwhelm the batting side that can of course hear these comments, too. As long as the comments are not inappropriate or rude, any vocal support players can give each other is valuable. This kind of support goes a long way toward settling down players who get tense during a match.

Most young players tend to get excited and nervous when waiting to bat. To help matters, have them sit in a group and watch the match as it progresses. Be with your players as much as possible to calm them and give them advice. Players can learn a great deal from observing, especially if you are there to highlight teaching points for them.

As players prepare to go to bat, give clear instructions, such as, "keep the run rate going" and "make sure you call loudly when you run between the wickets." Players should know exactly what you expect from them before they go into bat. This kind of "role clarity" particularly helps young players who might be unsure what to do in certain situations.

With regard to batting, a common question is, Should batsmen attack the bowling or try to be cautious? At the end of an innings, do you want to have wickets in hand, or should players go all guns blazing? Do you have batsmen who are aggressive batting with those who are defensive? When should you tell batsmen to rebuild an innings after a shaky start? What total is a good total? How do your players go about chasing down a large target?

If you're unsure how to answer any of these questions (and if you are, that's fine—an entire book could be written on these subjects!), simply ask other coaches or do some research. It's not vital to have all the answers, but it's useful to have an idea. Many of the details of cricket you will learn over time. In most cases common sense will get you through. It also helps to have some friendly, cricket-savvy parents to offer suggestions when you're in a tight spot.

After the Match

Regardless of what happens on match day, whether your team loses or wins, take the opportunity at the end of a match to teach respect for the officials and opposition. It's common practice for players to form a line after the match to shake the hands of everyone involved with making the match happen. Shaking hands and offering thanks should be requirements for your team. This kind of etiquette builds good spirit and a sense of sportsmanship among your players. To coach a team that wins a fair play award is truly a joy.

Above all, the keys to coaching are to help your team build skills, build character, and have a great time. At the end of a match, be positive no matter the outcome. Talk to your team about the good things in the match as well as the areas in which they need to improve, but always stay upbeat. Help players reflect on what they have accomplished and what they have yet to achieve. Sit down as a group and ask them what they did well and what they could have done better as a team. Be sure to highlight the great things your players did. The best time to hold this debriefing session is right after the match, sitting on the outfield. Never be harsh on a young team. Use the teaching strategy of asking questions. You can always lead their answers to the subjects you want to discuss.

Depending on the age of your players, in the event of a loss you might need to boost your team up by highlighting the positives of a match. Always be encouraging. Think back to chapter 1. At this level, your role is to develop young talent, not win all your cricket matches. The best coaches are not those with the most wins but those with a record of developing young players. Stay upbeat, put losses behind you, and help your team look ahead to the next match.

Developing Season and Practice Plans

With today's focus on fitness as an integral part of young players' development, cricket has become much more of a year-round sport, with players practicing in the off-season far more than they did twenty years ago. This being the case, it's important for coaches to thoroughly develop their season and practice plans. Preventing injuries, preparing for competition, and maintaining skill levels are now standard for young cricket players at all levels, and our practice plans must reflect that.

Season Plans

Generally speaking, you work on the technical in the off-season and the tactical in the on-season. That is, you focus on such things as *how* to bowl the ball, how to hit, and so on in the off-season, and focus more on *where* to bowl the ball, where to hit, and so on during the season itself. In cricket, a six-month season is usually preceded by a month's preseason in which outdoor practice helps transit between indoor practice and outdoor nets. But before this, there's a three-month time frame during which players work on the technical aspects of their game. Though this time is technically part of the "off" season, there's not much "off" about it if you want to keep your players in stride with the development of their peers. In the UK, this three-month period is January through March, and most young players will be getting into the nets at this time. Much of the training during this period is based on fitness work, cardiovascular work, speed-agility-quickness drills, and skill-based activities such as batting and bowling.

Encouraging young players to be fit is important, but don't neglect skills training by overemphasising fitness work. Too many coaches think that getting kids to run about, hop through rope ladders, and touch pretty-coloured

Coaching Tip

You have heard the phrase "practice makes perfect," but coaches know it's not that easy. In fact, *perfect* practice makes players closer to perfect. Precisely what your players practice makes all the difference. This is why you must carefully plan your practice sessions. If you have no goals, any road will get you there. Be smart about the sessions you run. If you allow players to practice poor habits, they'll take those habits into matches.

cones is in some way coaching cricket. It's not. If your time is short, don't waste valuable coaching minutes on such activities. Rather, plan in your SAQ drill work or general fitness work *around* your skills training sessions. Or perhaps use certain fitness sessions as part of a good warm-up. Yes, fitness needs to be part of your practice, but when you work on fitness, make these sessions cricket specific. That is, use the movements that players use in cricket skills so you are reinforcing what your players need. If you are unsure, always remember that to improve cricket, players need to do those cricket skills they need to play. You simply cannot beat batting and bowling for batsmen and bowlers.

Try to arrange regular (weekly) sessions for your squad so you can assess them, put them through their paces, and work skills with them. You need to reassess your players each year during the preseason. An early-developing player who was excellent one season might not be quite as good the next. The opposite might be true for a late-developing player. Don't base decisions on what you saw the season before. Regular monitoring of players is required if you want to truly understand your team and be fair to all.

Practice Plans

Setting a simple framework for practice plans helps you and your players measure and monitor progress. As part of developing youth players, a structured and progressive set of plans ensures that everyone knows if they are on track and properly prepared for the oncoming season. The structure also helps with expectation levels of all concerned.

Off-Season

The off-season covers the entire time from the end of a season until a month before the new season starts. It is a five-month period in which structured sessions should be formed. These sessions could be based on the entire five-month (or approximately 20-week) period but will usually be split into manageable segments. For illustrative purposes, we show a 10-week plan, but this could be any length of time you desire. A typical 10-week series of off-season practice sessions for youth cricket might look like what is shown in figure 11.1.

Again, the plan shown in the figure only gives you an idea of what your off-season plan could look like. You can add to this plan, tweak it, extend it,

Figure 11.1   Off-Season Practice Plan

	Practice focus	Description
Week 1	Nets	Assessment of players; allow all players to have an equal time with bat and ball, if required. Choose positions for players (batsmen, bowlers, wicket keepers, and all-rounders).
Week 2	Skill drills	Choose specific batting skills for all players to practice.
Week 3	Nets	Focus on the batting skills learned the week before.
Week 4	Skill drills	Choose batting and bowling skills for all players to practice
Week 5	Nets	Focus on the batting and bowling skills learned the week before.
Week 6	Fielding	Choose throwing and ground fielding skills for all players to practice; include general fitness drills.
Week 7	Skill drills	Choose batting and bowling skills for all players to practice.
Week 8	Nets	Focus on the batting and bowling skills learned the week before.
Week 9	Skill drills	Choose batting and bowling skills for all players to practice.
Week 10	Fielding	Choose throwing and ground fielding skills for all players to practice; include general fitness drills. Also focus on the batting and bowling skills learned the week before.

or alter it completely. The details of what you need to coach your players and work with them on is best determined by their skill levels and the standard at which they play. Very young players probably need far more basic coaching than those who have been playing a while. Also, the length of sessions should be varied according to age because older players have more stamina and higher levels of concentration.

Preseason

The preseason period is the month or so leading into the new season. During this time, weather permitting, your players are practicing outdoors and bringing together all the technical aspects of their off-season work. During the preseason everyone starts to get into the mindset of playing in competition. This is why the most important thing for you to think about during the preseason is providing your players with a smooth transition from skill (technical) into competition-related outcomes (tactical).

Generally, the closer you get to the season the more you should be thinking about teamwork, building rapport in your squad, getting bowlers to bowl straight, getting batsmen to hit the ball into gaps in the field, and so on, so that your team begins to align itself with what actually happens in matches. A typical four-week series of sessions in the preseason might look like what's shown in figure 11.2.

Figure 11.2   Preseason Practice Plan

	Practice focus	Description
Week 1	Nets	Regrooving cricket shots and using a bowling machine or throw downs. Bowlers to use target practice to groove areas to bowl in. Combative sessions in which batsmen try to either last against the bowlers (without getting out) or chase set run targets.
Week 2	Nets and square practice	Working toward goals such as being able to bowl six balls consistently in the same place, setting scenarios such as taking wickets or trying to score an amount of runs in a set number of deliveries that would be faced at various times during a match. Fielding practice and catching.
Week 3	Square practice	Setting field placing and having batsmen running between the wickets, while bowlers try to replicate match situations. Fielding practice and catching.
Week 4	Game practice	20 over, 30 over, or 40 over practice matches or scenarios. Situations to be assessed and feedback given.

The Season

During the season itself, focus on running practice sessions that reflect match situations. Note that many of the drills we have included in this book are designed to support skill work while allowing players to develop a feel for those skills in a fun yet realistic environment.

Practice sessions in season might be run-through matches in which the fun element is paramount. During play, stop the game to highlight the things that work well and those that do not, and then start play back up again. By using game-based drills as practice sessions, you introduce less of a fear factor for cricket regarding the game's result. Kids focus more on getting better at the technical stuff, and less on who wins and loses. This mindset carries over into real matches. Plus, once players know they can execute the skills you have set up, they can be more relaxed when they play in match competition.

Make time during practice sessions and after matches for reflection and feedback. Reflection is an excellent starting point for your young players to begin the process of self-assessment. Questions such as "What did we do well today?" and "How could we have done better?" go a long way toward helping players with their honest appraisal of themselves. Team gatherings can also be excellent for getting everyone excited and feeling part of the team. Let everyone have the chance to say something.

During the season you can plan for and monitor team progress by setting specific team goals and measuring progress toward them. If something isn't measured, it isn't managed, so make sure you have a way of measuring your practice sessions and matches. Are fewer wides bowled? Or more boundaries hit? Have they dropped less catches? Were more runs taken?

When you get your players to focus on doing the small things right, the big picture becomes more clear for them. If bowlers focus on bowling straight, the outcome is more wickets. When batsmen focus on running hard between the wickets, the outcome is a higher number of total runs. These are individual focuses that you can drill down into so that players can have their own goals within a game or a session and find success. Find ways to give all players a target or a goal. You might use paired targets in which you link two players and set them the goal of taking a certain amount of catches between them, or two bowlers trying to total more wickets than they did the season before.

As coach, there's a great deal you can do to get your players to take responsibility for their own development. Make practice sessions progressive, realistic, and above all fun. Create small goals that are attainable. Let players have many "wins" in their practices. Build an atmosphere of success. Teach players to try new things and make mistakes. Encourage a team spirit in which everyone wants to play for each other. Go for quality over quantity in training. Practice doesn't make perfect—it makes permanent. Only perfect practice makes perfect, so don't let yourself or your players get lazy. Try to make every minute of each practice session a quality minute.

Appendix A

Related Checklists and Forms

This appendix contains checklists and forms referred to in the text. They pertain to safety and legal issues relevant to running a cricket programme. Some of them should be of use to you at the beginning of your season or in the preseason, whereas others should be copied and brought to every practice and match over the season. The facilities and equipment checklist should be filled out ahead of every match. You may reproduce and use these checklists and forms as needed.

Facilities and Equipment Checklist

Outfield and Square

☐ Any sprinkler heads, taps, and openings are at grass level.

☐ The outfield is free of toxic substances (lime, fertilizer, and so on).

☐ The outfield is free of low spots or ruts.

☐ The outfield is free of debris that can cause injury.

☐ No rocks or cement slabs are on the outfield.

☐ The outfield is free of protruding pipes, wires, and lines.

☐ Sightscreens, where available, are correctly lined up with the pitch you are playing on.

☐ The field is not too wet, which can be dangerous for stable footing and cause fielders to slip.

☐ The field is not too dry or hard (protecting players who dive or fall).

☐ The outfield lines and pitch are well marked with any required distance markers for fielders clearly marked for umpires and players to see.

☐ Stumps are of the correct height and bails available.

☐ The correct lines are marked for the crease and are clearly visible.

☐ The distance between the stumps from wicket to wicket (pitch length) is correct for the age group playing.

☐ The cricket balls are the right size for the age group playing.

Outside Playing Area

☐ The edge of the playing field is at least 6 feet (1.8 m) from trees, walls, fences, and cars.

☐ Nearby buildings are protected (by fences, walls) from possible damage during play.

☐ Storage sheds and facilities are locked.

☐ The playground area (ground surface and equipment) is in safe condition.

☐ The fences or walls lining the area are in good repair.

☐ Paths and steps are without cracks, separations, or raised concrete.

From ASEP, 2010, *Coaching Youth Cricket* (Champaign, IL: Human Kinetics).

❑ Scorers, scoreboard, and umpires are available and have all the equipment required to do the job.

Equipment

❑ Boundaries are marked clearly with a rope, line, or flags.

❑ Batting helmets are in good condition with no cracks.

❑ All players are wearing correct footwear; laces are tied.

❑ Practice clothing and uniforms fit appropriately; hats don't obstruct vision.

❑ Batting helmets and abdominal guards are available for all players.

❑ Pads, gloves, and other protective equipment fit correctly.

Spectators

❑ Areas for spectators are clearly marked.

❑ Spectators have adequate protection from flying objects.

From ASEP, 2010, *Coaching Youth Cricket* (Champaign, IL: Human Kinetics).

Informed Consent Form

I hereby give my permission for _____
to participate in _____ during the season
beginning on _____. Further, I authorise the school or club
to provide emergency treatment of any injury or illness my child may experience if qualified medical personnel consider treatment necessary and perform
the treatment. This authorisation is granted only if I cannot be reached and
reasonable effort has been made to do so.

Parent or guardian: _____

Address: _____

Phone: (   ) _____ Other phone: (   ) _____

Additional contact in case of emergency: _____

_____

Relationship to athlete: _____ Phone: (   ) _____

Family doctor: _____ Phone: (   ) _____

Medical conditions (e.g., allergies, chronic illness):

_____

_____

My child and I are aware that participating in _____
is a potentially hazardous activity. We assume all risks associated with participation in this sport, including but not limited to falls, contact with other
participants, the effects of the weather, traffic, and other reasonable-risk conditions associated with the sport. All such risks to my child are known and
appreciated by my child and me.

We understand this informed consent form and agree to its conditions.

Player's signature: _____
Date: _____

Parent's or guardian's signature: _____
Date: _____

From ASEP, 2010, *Coaching Youth Cricket* (Champaign, IL: Human Kinetics).

Injury Report Form

Date of injury: _____ Time: _____ a.m./p.m.

Location: _____

Athlete's name: _____

Age: _____ Date of birth: _____

Type of injury: _____

Anatomical area involved: _____

Cause of injury: _____

_____

_____

Extent of injury: _____

_____

_____

Person administering first aid (name): _____

First aid administered: _____

_____

Other treatment administered: _____

_____

Referral action: _____

_____

_____

Signature of person administering first aid: _____

Date: _____

From ASEP, 2010, *Coaching Youth Cricket* (Champaign, IL: Human Kinetics).

Emergency Information Card

Player's name: _____ Date of birth: _____

Address: _____

Phone: (   ) _____

Contact Information

Parent's or guardian's name: _____

Address: _____

Phone: (   ) _____ Other phone: (   ) _____

Additional contact's name: _____

Relationship to athlete: _____

Address: _____

Phone: (   ) _____ Other phone: (   ) _____

Medical Information

Physician's name: _____

Address: _____

Phone: (   ) _____

Is your child allergic to any drugs?   *YES*   *NO*

If so, what? _____

Does your child have any allergies (e.g., bee stings, dust)? _____

_____

Does your child have any of the following?   *asthma*   *diabetes*   *epilepsy*

Is your child currently taking medication?   *YES*   *NO*

If so, what for? _____

Does your child wear contact lenses?   *YES*   *NO*

Is there additional information we should know about your child's health or
     physical condition?   *YES*   *NO*

If yes, please explain: _____

_____

_____

Parent's or guardian's signature: _____

Date: _____

From ASEP, 2010, *Coaching Youth Cricket* (Champaign, IL: Human Kinetics).

Emergency Response Card

Be prepared to give the following information to a medical professional.

(*Note:* Do not hang up first. Let the medical professional hang up first.)

Caller's name: _____

Telephone number from which the call is being made:_____

Reason for call: _____

How many people are injured: _____

Condition of victim(s): _____

_____

_____

First aid being given: _____

_____

Location: _____

Address: _____

City: _____

Directions (e.g., cross streets, landmarks, entrance access):

From ASEP, 2010, *Coaching Youth Cricket* (Champaign, IL: Human Kinetics).

Appendix B

Cricket Terms

arm ball—A ball bowled by a slow bowler that has no spin on it and so does not turn as expected but stays on a straight line ("goes on with the arm").

asking rate—The runs required per over for a team to win; mostly relevant in a limited overs match. Could also be a one-day match, 20/20 match, or overs left in a longer version of the game.

ball—The ball is red for first class and most club cricket or white for one-day matches. Either ball weighs 5-1/2 ounces for adult club cricket, 5 ounces for women's cricket, and 4-3/4 ounces for junior cricket.

ball tampering—The illegal action of changing the condition of the ball by artificial means, usually by scuffing the surface, picking or lifting the seam of the ball, or applying substances other than sweat or saliva.

bat pad—A fielding position close to the batsman designed to catch balls that pop up off the bat, often via the batsman's pads

batter—Another word for batsman, first used as long ago as 1773.

beamer—A ball that does not bounce (usually accidentally) and passes the batsman at or about head height. If aimed straight at the batsman by a fast bowler, this is a very dangerous delivery that's generally frowned upon.

blob—A score of 0. Also known as a duck.

bouncer—A short-pitched ball that passes the batsman at chest or head height. Also called a bumper.

boundary—The perimeter of a cricket field, or the act of the batsman scoring a four or a six (e.g. "Tendulkar hammered three boundaries").

box—An abdominal protector worn by batsmen and male wicket keepers. It is also an old term for a fielder in the gully region.

bump ball—A ball that is played off the bat almost instantly into the ground and is caught by a fielder. Often has the appearance of being a clean catch.

bumper—A short-pitched ball that passes the batsman at chest or head height. Also called a bouncer.

bye—A run scored when the batsman does not touch the ball with either bat or body. First recorded in the 1770s.

"carry your bat"—An opening batsman who remains not out at the end of a completed innings (i.e., when all teammates are out).

chest-on—A term used to describe a bowler who delivers the ball with chest facing the batsman, as opposed to being side-on. However, it's actually where the back foot points that dictates what type of bowler a person is. If it points straight down the pitch they are chest-on (or front–on); if it points at 45 degrees, they are mid-way or 'semi'; and if it is at 90 degrees they are side-on. The idea is to align the top and bottom half to avoid a 'mixed action', which is where the hips point one way and the shoulders point another.

chinaman—A ball bowled by a left-arm slow bowler that turns into the right-handed batsman, in effect a left-arm legspinner; named after Puss Achong.

chin music—Fast bowlers aiming the ball at the batsman's head. The term originated in the Caribbean.

chucker—Another term for a bowler who throws the ball.

closing the face—Turning the face of the bat inward and, in doing so, hitting the ball to the leg side.

corridor of uncertainty—A term beloved by commentators that describes an area just outside the batsmen's off stump where they are unsure whether they have to leave or play the ball.

cow corner—An unconventional fielding position, more commonly found in the lower reaches of the game, on the midwicket/long-on boundary. The term is thought to have originated at Dulwich College, where there was the corner of a field containing livestock on that edge of the playing area. Fielders were dispatched to the "cow corner."

cross bat—A cross-batted shot is where the batsman holds the bat horizontally when striking the ball. Examples of cross-batted shots include hooks, pulls, and cuts.

dead ball—A ball from which no runs can be scored or wickets taken. The term was coined in 1798.

declaration—When the batting side ends their innings before all their players are out.

dolly—An easy catch.

doosra—A Hindi/Urdu word that means "second" or "other"; the doosra is the off-spinner's version of the googly, delivered out of the back of the hand and turning away from the right-hand batsman.

drifter—A delivery bowled by an offspinner that curves away from a right-hander and then carries straight on instead of turning; also called a floater.

duck—A score of 0. Also known as a blob.

economy rate—The average number of runs a bowler concedes per over.

extras—Runs not scored by batsmen. There are four common extras: byes, leg byes, wides, and no-balls. In Australia these are known as sundries.

featherbed—A batsmen-friendly pitch with little life for the bowlers. Often found in Antigua.

flipper—A delivery variation for the legspinner that appears to be pitching short, but the ball skids on quickly and often results in the batter being bowled or leg-before wicket. It is a delivery that is used sparingly.

full toss—A low ball that reaches the batsmen without bouncing. Note that above waist height it becomes a beamer.

gardening—The act of the batsman repairing indentations in the pitch, made by the ball or studs, with the bat. More likely to happen when a ball has just whistled past the nose or scooted by the ankle as a reaction to the surprise that the ball has behaved badly.

giving the charge—When a batsman leaves a crease to attack the ball, usually against a slow bowler. By doing this the batsman can convert a good-length ball into a half-volley.

good length—The ideal length that the bowler aims for, forcing the batter to be indecisive as whether to play forward or back.

googly—The legspinner's variation that turns into the right-hander and away from the left-hander.

grubber—A ball that hardly bounces. Also called a shooter.

half volley—A ball that is the perfect length for driving; fuller than a good length but not a full-toss.

handled the ball—A phrase meaning that if batsmen deliberately touch the ball with their hands, they can be given out. Michael Vaughan fell victim to this in India in the 2002-03 tour in Bangalore.

heavy ball—When a delivery is quicker than it looks and hits the bat harder or higher than expected.

hit the ball twice—If batsmen deliberately strike the ball twice to gain runs they can be given out. However, the batsman can knock the ball away from the stumps with the bat.

in-ducker—An in-swinging delivery that moves into the batsman very late. Wasim Akram produced deadly versions with the older ball.

inside out, turning the batsman—A batsman aims to leg, but the ball goes past the off, and the batsman is forced to play the ball open-chested.

inside-out shot—A stroke in which the batsman moves toward the leg side and hits a ball around leg stump into the off side.

jaffa—A delivery that is too good for the batsman and leaves him or her groping hopelessly at thin air or (as the bowler will hope) dismisses the batsman.

leading edge—When the batsman mis-hits the ball and edges it forward in the opposite direction to which he or she was attempting to play.

leg-before wicket (LBW)—One of the game's more complex rules, but at its simplest, it means you cannot be out if the ball pitched *outside* the line of leg stump; you cannot be out if the ball hits you outside the line off stump unless you are offering no stroke. Aside from that, if the ball hits you in line, the only decision the umpire has to make is whether the ball is going on to hit the stumps.

leg-bye—When the ball deflects off the pad and the batsmen run. A shot must be offered to the ball. Leg-byes do not count against the bowler.

leg-break/spin—When the ball pitches and turns from leg to off for a right-hander.

leg-cutter—A ball that cuts and moves away from the batsman toward the off side (if the batsman is right-handed).

leg side—The area of the pitch behind the batsman's legs.

length—Where the ball pitches down the wicket. Lengths can be generally short, full, or good.

lifter—A ball that rises unexpectedly.

line—The line of attack the bowler employs when bowling.

lollipop—A really easy ball to hit.

long hop—A ball that pitches short, sits up, and "begs" to be hit.

loop—The flight of the ball.

maiden—An over in which no runs that are attributable to the bowler are scored (byes or leg-byes may be scored in this over, though, because these don't count against the bowler).

middle—To hit the ball from the meat of the bat. "To middle it" is to connect really well. Middle is also the centre of the field, where most of the action takes place.

minefield—A difficult batting track. The pitch is in such a state of disrepair that it is almost impossible to play "proper" shots because the ball is popping up everywhere.

nervous nineties—The psychological pressure on batsmen knowing they are approaching a century.

net run rate—A system for separating sides who finish on level points in multiteam tournaments.

new ball—Can usually be taken every 80 overs. The advantage is to quick bowlers who have a shiny and bouncy ball but conversely can result in an increase in scoring rate because the ball comes off the bat faster.

nick—A faint edge off the bat.

nightwatchman—A non batsman promoted up the order toward the end of a day's play with the idea of shielding a recognised batsman in the final overs.

no-ball—An illegitimate delivery, usually when the bowler has overstepped on the front crease.

nurdle—The batsman nudging the ball around and into gaps.

obstruction—When the batsman wilfully blocks or distracts a fielder to prevent a catch being made or a run-out being effected.

occupy the crease—When a batsman stays at the wicket but scores slowly, often with the intention of playing out for a draw.

off-break/spin—A ball turning into the right-hander from off to leg (from left to right).

off-cutter—An off-break delivered at speed.

off the mark—When the batsman scores his or her first run.

off side—The side of the pitch that is to the batsman's right (if right-handed) or left (if left-handed).

on side—The area of the pitch behind the batsman's legs (same as the leg side).

on the up—Making contact with the ball before it reaches the top of the bounce: hitting the ball on the rise. Viv Richards was a prominent exponent.

out—There are 10 possible ways of being out: bowled, caught, hit wicket, LBW, stumped, timed out, handling the ball, obstruction, hit the ball twice, and run out.

To be "retired out" is gaining in currency and popularity and counts as a dismissal, in contrast to "retired hurt."

outside edge—When the ball hits the edge of the bat that is furthest from the body.

outswing—When the ball swings away from the batsman and toward the slips.

paddle—A sweep shot.

pair—When a batsman gets a duck in both innings.

pinch-hitters—Lower-order batsmen promoted in the lineup to try to hit up a few quick runs. Used mostly when a team is chasing a huge total in a one-dayer, the thinking being that a few quick runs will reduce the asking rate; and if the pinch-hitter gets out, the specialist batsmen are still around.

pitch—The bounce of the ball: "It pitches on a good length." Also the cut strip in the centre of the field of play.

play on—When a batsman hits the ball, but the ball goes on to hit the stumps and the batsman is bowled.

plumb—When batsmen are clearly leg-before wicket, even at full speed, they are said to be plumb in front.

pudding—A slow, stodgy pitch difficult to score quickly on.

pull—A back-foot leg-side shot distinct from the hook because the pull is played to a ball that hasn't risen as high.

return crease—Parallel white lines pointing down the pitch on either side of the stumps. A bowler's back foot must land inside this area or else a no-ball is called.

retire—To postpone or end one's innings, either voluntarily through boredom when you're simply too good for the opposition, or involuntarily and in agony when a nasty fast bowler has taken a pound of flesh.

reverse sweep—The epitome of the type of shot you will not find in the MCC coaching manual. This stroke is played by dropping to one knee and reversing one's hands, so that you can swing the ball from leg to off rather than the more natural off to leg. The reverse is a handy stroke for beating conventional fields in a one-day game but has its drawbacks as well—just ask Mike Gatting.

reverse swing—When the ball is 50 overs old and the pitch is as flat as a pancake, this phenomenon is often a bowling side's saving grace. First mastered by the Pakistani quicks of the 1980s and 1990s, it involves sideways movement of the ball through the air that is contrary to your average everyday laws of physics.

rip—Big turn for a spin bowler, especially a legspinner, who can use the whole action of the wrist to impart maximum revolutions on the ball. Shane Warne, consequently, bowls a lot of "rippers."

ring field—A standard fielding arrangement with players positioned in a circle all around the bat saving the single.

roll—To flatten the playing surface with a heavy rolling device. At the end of an innings, the side about to start their innings will be offered the choice of a heavy or light roller.

roller—A heavy rolling device designed to flatten the surface of the pitch

rope—Used to mark the perimeter of the field. If the ball crosses or hits the rope, a boundary will be signalled.

rough—The area of a pitch that is scuffed up and loosened by the action of a bowler running through in the follow-through. Usually this will be situated a foot or so (.3 m) outside leg stump and consequently becomes a tasty target for spin bowlers, who can exploit the extra turn to make life a misery for batsmen.

run-chase—Generally the fourth innings of a first-class or test match, and the latter stages of a one-day game, when the match situation has been reduced to a set figure for victory, within a set time or maximum number of overs.

run-rate—Of particular importance in a one-day game, this is the average number of runs scored per over and is used as a guide to a team's progress.

run-up—The preparatory strides taken by bowlers as they steady themselves for delivery. Also the area in which they perform said action.

runner—A player who is called on by a batsman who might otherwise need to retire hurt. This player is required to wear the same padding and stands at square leg or the nonstriker's end to perform the duty of running between the wickets. Often the cause of endless confusion and inevitable run-outs.

seam—The ridge of stitching that holds the two halves of a ball together and causes deviation off the pitch when the ball lands. Seam bowlers, as opposed to swing bowlers, rely on movement off the pitch rather than through the air.

shoulder arms—The description of when a batsman decides that rather than risk being dismissed from a ball, he or she lifts the bat high above the shoulder to attempt to keep the bat and hands out of harm's way.

Shooter—A ball that hardly bounces. Also called a grubber.

sitter—The easiest, most innocuous, and undroppable catch that a fielder can receive. To drop one of these is to invite a whole world of pain from the crowd and constant embarrassment from the giant replay screen.

slob—Also known as the world's best slower ball, created by Ian Pont. The delivery has no rotation on it and is bowled out of the palm of the hand with a push. It deceives the batsman in flight by dropping like a stone during the last part of its journey. It looks like a normal delivery in the hand but is in fact held only with the two fingers of the bowling hand.

standing back/standing up—Where a wicket keeper positions for a particular bowler. The keeper stands back for fast bowlers and stands up for spinners.

stock ball—A bowler's regular delivery, offering minimum risk with little chance of runs or wickets. To get away with a slower ball, they need a stock ball to lull the batsman into a false sense of security.

strike rate—The number of runs a batsman scores per 100 balls; the number of deliveries a bowler needs to take his or her wickets.

sundries—Australian word for extras.

swing—A ball that curves through the air as opposed to off the seam.

tailender—Players who come in toward the end of an innings, generally numbers 8, 9, 10, and 11, who are not noted for their batting prowess (although ideally they can bowl a bit by way of compensation).

throwing—To deliver the ball with a arm that flexes at the elbow at point of delivery, thereby enabling extra spin to be imparted for a slow bowler, or extra pace for a quick bowler. A topic of endless debate.

ton—A century (100 runs by a single batsman in one innings).

track—The pitch; the cut strip in the centre of the field of play.

twelfth man—A substitute fielder for the chosen 11. If called on to play, the 12th man is permitted to field wherever needed but can neither bat nor bowl.

two-paced—A wicket that is beginning to break up, usually after three or four days of a Test match, and so produces some deliveries that leap off a length, and others that sneak through at shin-height.

V—The arc between mid-off and mid-on in which batsmen who play straight (in accordance with the MCC coaching manual) tend to score the majority of their runs. Modern aggressive players, such as Virender Sehwag, tend to prefer the V between point and third man.

wagon-wheel—A circular graph or line-drawing depicting the region in which a batsman has scored runs.

walk—The improbable act of batsmen giving themselves out without waiting for an umpire's decision. Adam Gilchrist famously did this against Sri Lanka in the semifinal of the 2003 World Cup. Mike Atherton, equally famous, did not at Trent Bridge in 1998 en route to a match-winning 98 not out against South Africa.

wicket—One of those ubiquitous words central to the game of cricket. The word can be used to describe the 22 yards between the stumps, the stumps collectively (bails included), the act of hitting these stumps and so dismissing the batsman, and perversely, the act of not being out.

wide—A delivery that pitches too far away from the batsman and so proves impossible to score off. The umpire will signal this by stretching arms out horizontally; an extra is added to the total, and the ball will be bowled again.

wrist spin—The version of spin bowling in which the revolutions on the ball are imparted via a flick of the wrist rather than a tweak of the fingers. As a general rule, a right-arm wristspinner's action turns the ball from leg to off (legspin), whereas a left-armer turns it from off to leg.

Wrong 'un—Australian term for a googly: a legspinner's delivery that turns in the opposite direction, from off to leg.

Yorker—A full-pitched delivery aimed at the batsman's toes or the base of the stumps. If the ball is swinging, these can be the most lethal delivery in the game, as perfected by Waqar Younis in his pomp.

Zooter—A spin-bowling variation, first devised by Shane Warne. This is a delivery that snakes out of the hand with little or no spin imparted and so deceives through its very ordinariness. Some question whether the delivery has ever existed, for it could be another of Warne's mind games to keep opponents on their toes.

Appendix C

15 Game-Based Drills

In this appendix you'll find 15 game-based drills to use in your cricket programme. These drills differ from those in chapters 7 through 9 in that they focus on creating game-like scenarios, allowing for both attacking and defensive situations, and setting up competition between players while under the kind of pressure they would experience in real matches. I suggest using these drills during practices to keep motivation high and make the sport fun for your young players. The game-like drills are designed to give you control over how you manipulate what is taught and learned in your practices. Be as creative as you wish. As with the drills in the chapters, you should modify these drills as necessary to suit your purposes and your players.

Quick Runs, Safe Catches

Objectives: To acquire and develop batting and fielding skills; reduce the amount of runs scored when fielding and complete the allocated amount of catches; to increase opportunities to score runs when batting

What You'll Need: Players in groups of 8, 1 tennis ball per group, 3 cones per group, 2 sets of stumps per group, 2 bats per group

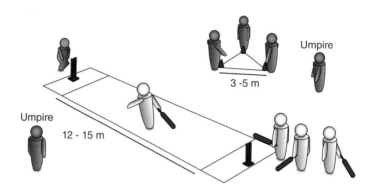

Procedure: Players organise as shown, and groups are further broken down into a batting team of four players and a fielding team of three players. The first batter begins running to the far crease and back; once he has done this, the next player for the batting team takes over; this repeats for all players in line. When the batter sets off to run, fielders begin to throw the ball to one another underarm in a clockwise direction and to catch the ball in a close catching position. Fielders must complete 20 catches as quickly as possible. Once the 20th catch is complete, the ball is thrown to the wicket keeper, who touches the ball on the stumps and shouts "stop!" The coach or teacher adds the amount of runs scored within the time that it took for the fielding team to make 20 catches. Runs are deducted if the batters do not slide their bat over the line. The team with the most runs is the winner.

Key Points
- When running, players should make loud and clear calls (e.g., Yes! No! Wait! Run straight! Run hard!).
- Runners approach the ends in a low, balanced position and reach out and slide the bat over the line.
- Runners face the ball when turning and drive up from a low position.
- Fielders maintain a relaxed stance with feet about shoulder-width apart, knees bent, and weight on balls of the feet.
- Fielders' hands should be together with fingers pointing down, making a big catching area, when preparing to catch the ball. Give with the ball.
- Fielder's heads are level with eyes on the ball.

Variations: Increase or decrease the running area; increase or decrease the throwing area; add more runs per batter; add more catches; add fielders; require two batters to run at a time; use a bigger ball; catch one-handed; change direction on throws.

Pairs Batting

Objectives: To acquire and develop batting, bowling, and fielding skills; to select and apply skills and tactics to score more runs; to reduce the amount of runs scored when fielding; to evaluate and improve execution by following instructions; to understand the importance of being fit in order to run effectively between the wickets

What You'll Need: Players in groups of 12, 1 soft ball per group, 1 set of stumps per group, 2 bats per group

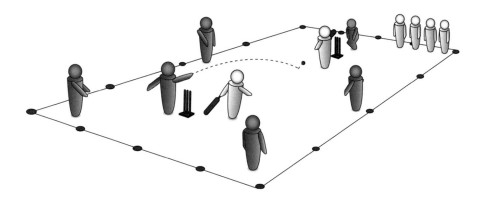

Procedure: Break the group down into two equal teams, as shown. There should be three pairs of players per team. Those pairs bat for two overs each. There are no boundaries, and all scores have to be run. Batters may be bowled, caught, or run out. Five runs will be deducted from the score for every wicket lost. Fielders will bowl one over each for a completed innings before teams rotate. The pair with the highest score wins.

Key Points

- When batting, ensure the grip is correct and that players are in a relaxed, balanced stance.
- Batters should watch the ball and apply the correct shot while trying to keep the ball down.
- Batters should call loudly and early when attempting runs.
- When fielding, react to the ball with hands ready and watch the ball into your hands.
- After the fielder has secured the ball, he adopts the throwing position and aims at the base of the stumps.
- The fielder backs fielders up to prevent additional runs.
- When bowling, players use the correct grip, and the front arm pushes out toward the target. The bowling hand pushes out and down.
- Bowlers should use a full arm swing with shoulder rotation.
- When bowling, the back leg steps through.
- Bowlers should keep their head steady and concentrate on line and length.

Variations: Increase or decrease boundaries of the playing area; increase or decrease the number of fielders; run every delivery that is played; hit from a tee; vary the type of serves used; bowl off side or leg side only.

Pairs Cricket

Objectives: To acquire and develop batting, bowling, and fielding skills; to select and apply skills and tactics to score more runs; to reduce the amount of runs scored when fielding and to identify where batters are hitting the ball; to evaluate and improve performance by observing other team members and following instructions; to understand the importance of being fit in order to run effectively between the wickets

What You'll Need: Players in groups of 8, 1 tennis ball per group, 2 sets of stumps per group, 2 bats per group

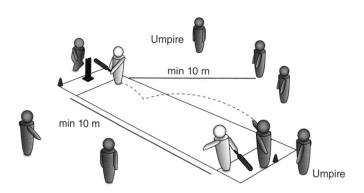

Procedure: Break groups down into pairs, as shown. In pairs, players bat, bowl, keep wicket, and field on the off side and leg side for two overs for each pair. Players rotate after two overs. Runs can be scored in the usual manner, including boundaries and extras. Wide deliveries count as two runs, but the ball will not be bowled again. Runs can be deducted each time a batter is out. Scores start at 200. Bonus runs can be awarded for taking a catch or running a batter out or bowling or stumping a batter out. The pair with the highest overall score once the rotation is complete wins.

Key Points
- When batting, ensure the grip is correct and that batters are in a relaxed, balanced stance.
- Batters should watch the ball and apply the correct shot, keeping the ball down.
- When fielding, players react to the ball with hands ready and watch the ball into their hands.
- After fielders secure the ball, they adopt the throwing position, aiming at the base of the stumps.
- The fielder backs fielders up to prevent additional runs.
- Runners make loud and clear calls (Yes! No! Wait! Run straight! Run hard!)
- Runners approach the ends in a low and balanced position, reaching out and sliding the bat over the line.
- Runners face the ball when turning and drive up from a low position.

Variations: Increase or decrease boundaries of the playing area; increase or decrease the number of fielders; batters hit from a tee; use different serves; use full equipment and a hard ball.

Full-Version Longball

Objectives: To acquire and develop batting, bowling, and fielding skills; to select and apply skills and tactics to score more runs while batting by hitting the ball into gaps and only running from the baseline when necessary; to reduce runs being scored by hitting the opponent with the ball; to evaluate and improve execution by observing other team members and the opposition perform and by listening to and following instructions

What You'll Need: Players in groups of 20, 1 soft ball per group, 1 cone per group, 1 set of stumps per group, 1 bat per group

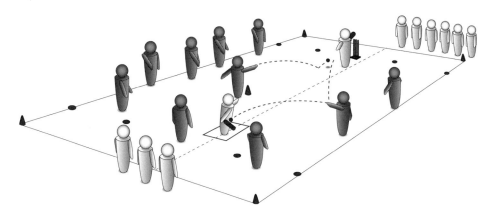

Procedure: Break groups down into two teams of 10, as shown. For the batting team, one player is at bat, three players position to catch loose balls, and the remaining players line up behind the batter, a safe distance away. The coach serves the ball to the batter, who hits the ball and then runs in an attempt to reach the safe zone and back to score a point. Fielders field the ball and attempt to hit the player with the ball as she runs. If the player is hit then she is out, and the teams switch. If a batting player reaches the safe zone she can decide to stay there or return immediately. A stop in the safe zone and return later earns 1 point, and an immediate return earns 3 points. The team with the most points after a set time is the winner.

Key Points
- When batting, ensure the grip is correct and that the player has assumed a relaxed and balanced stance with eyes on the ball.
- The batter should apply the correct shot and try to keep the ball down.
- When fielding, react to the ball with hands ready; watch the ball into the hands.
- After the fielder has secured the ball, she should adopt the throwing position and aim at the base of the stumps.
- The fielder should back fielders up to prevent additional runs.

Variations: Increase or decrease the size of the playing area; increase or decrease the number of fielders; hit the ball off a tee; throw or catch weak-handed.

Cricket Circuit

Objectives: To acquire and develop batting and fielding skills and to evaluate and improve execution by observing other team members and the opposition perform and by listening to and following instructions

What You'll Need: Players in groups of 14, 9 tennis balls per group, 6 cones per group, 4 bats per group

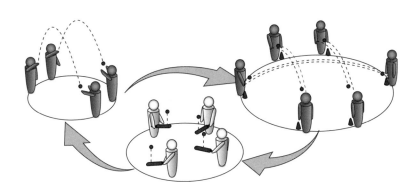

Procedure: Groups organise as shown and work in stations to practice close catching, bat control by bat tapping, and high catching; groups stay a set time at each station and then rotate to start at a new station.

Key Points
- When catching, players should be in a relaxed stance with feet about shoulder-width apart, knees bent, and weight on balls of their feet.
- When catching, players' hands are together with fingers pointing down to provide a big catching area. Palms point at the ball for high catches.
- Catchers' heads are level and eyes are on the ball. "Give" with the ball.
- When bat tapping, players hold the bat with both hands on the bat handle and watch the ball onto the bat with head steady.
- When bat tapping, players maintain balance when hitting the ball.

Variations: Increase or decrease the size of station areas; catch one-handed; add more balls; use bigger balls; add another station, such as agility, balance, or coordination exercises; keep individual scores and team scores.

Cricket Rounders

Objectives: To acquire and develop batting, fielding, and communicating skills; to select and apply skills and tactics to score more runs; to reduce the amount of runs scored when fielding; to evaluate and improve performance by observing other team members and following instructions

What You'll Need: Players in groups of 16, 1 tennis ball per group, 7 sets of stumps per group, 7 bats per group

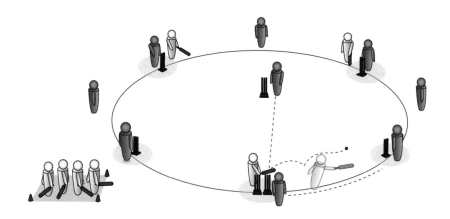

Procedure: Break groups down into two teams. A player in the centre of the playing area serves the ball underarm with one bounce to the batter of the batting team, who is standing at the crease; the remaining batters position at the other stumps or stand in line outside the playing area, a safe distance away. Fielders position around the playing area. The batter hits the ball and runs to first base or more, depending on where the ball is hit. To complete a run, a batter must successfully reach fourth base; if successful, he then joins the back of the line. Batters can be caught, bowled, or run out; once out, they join the back of the line. Fielders attempt to retrieve the ball and throw it to the nearest base fielder or to a base fielder where there's a chance of a run out. An innings can be a timed innings or until all are out. The team with the most runs wins.

Key Points

- When batting, ensure the grip is correct and that players are in a relaxed, balanced stance.
- Batters watch the ball and apply the correct shot, keeping the ball down.
- When fielding, players react to the ball with the hands ready and watch the ball into their hands.
- After the fielder has secured the ball, she adopts the throwing position and aims at the base of the stumps.
- The fielder backs fielders up to prevent additional runs.
- Runners make loud, clear calls.
- Runners run straight and hard, approaching the base in a low, balanced position.
- Runners reach out and slide their bat over the line near the base.

Variations: Increase or decrease the size of the base area; increase or decrease the number of fielders; add another base; use the weak hand when fielding; batters hit off a tee.

Diamond Cricket

Objectives: To acquire and develop batting and fielding skills; to select and apply skills and tactics to score more runs while only playing at balls that are necessary; to reduce the amount of runs scored; to evaluate and improve execution by observing other team members and following instructions

What You'll Need: Players in groups of 16, 1 tennis ball per group, 4 sets of stumps per group, 4 bats per group

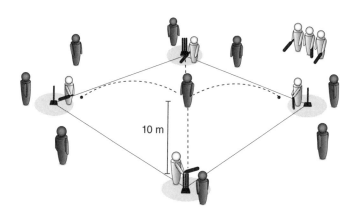

Procedure: Break teams down into two teams of eight, as shown. A player in the centre of the playing area bowls at any of the four batters at each corner; the remaining batters stand in line outside the playing area, a safe distance away. Fielders position around the playing area and retrieve balls hit by the batsmen and return them to the bowler so she can bowl the next ball. All batters run counterclockwise to the next set of stumps (as in baseball to the next "base") while the ball is being fielded. Batters can be caught, bowled, or run out. One run is given each time a successful rotation of all the stumps is made. Teams change sides after all batters are out. The team with the most runs wins.

Key Points
- When batting, ensure the grip is correct and that players are in a relaxed, balanced stance.
- Batters watch the ball and apply the correct shot, keeping the ball down.
- When fielding, players react to the ball with the hands ready and watch the ball into their hands.
- After the fielder has secured the ball, she adopts the throwing position and aims at the base of the stumps.
- The fielder should back fielders up to prevent additional runs.

Variations: Increase or decrease boundary size of playing area; increase or decrease number of fielders; batters hit from a tee; bowlers use different serves.

Beat the Catches

Objectives: To acquire and develop close catching skills and running between the wicket skills; to run hard and turn from a low position; to decrease the runs scored by throwing the ball quickly between teammates; to evaluate and improve, following instructions and analysing execution; to identify what type of fitness they are employing and how their bodies feel after running between the wickets

What You'll Need: Players in groups of 10, 2 stumps per group, 1 tennis ball per group, 5 bats per group

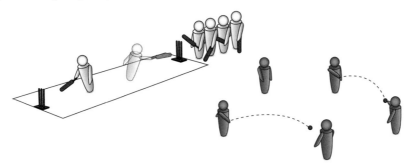

Procedure: Break groups down into two teams of five, as shown. On command, the first player in line on the batting team starts from a batting stance position and runs across the area and back, sliding the bat over the designated lines. Upon the first player's return, the second player in line performs the exercise. This continues until all have completed one run. At the same time the first player on the batting team begins his run, the fielding team, lined up in two staggered lines, throws the ball underarm to one another and back. They try to make as many catches as possible in the time it takes the batting team to complete their runs. Teams swap over after a completed innings. The team that has made the most catches wins.

Key Points
- When catching, players are in a relaxed stance with feet about shoulder-width apart, knees bent, and weight on balls of the feet.
- When catching, the players' hands are together, with fingers pointing down to provide a big catching area.
- Catchers' heads are level as they watch the ball. "Give" with the ball.
- Runners make loud and clear calls (Yes! No! Wait! Run straight! Run hard!)
- Runners approach the ends in a low, balanced position, reaching out and sliding the bat over the line.
- Runners should face the ball when turning and drive up from a low position.

Variations: Increase throwing distance; increase or decrease running distance; vary direction and height of throws; add another ball; use bigger ball; time the game; catch one-handed or with the weak hand; increase the number of runs.

Stopping Two

Objectives: To run between the wicket skills and intercept the ball and throw; to prevent runs by attacking the ball and throwing the ball in flat and fast; to evaluate and improve by following instructions; to understand importance of fitness

What You'll Need: Players in groups of 10, 1 tennis ball per group, 1 cone per group, 2 sets of stumps per group, at least 2 bats per group

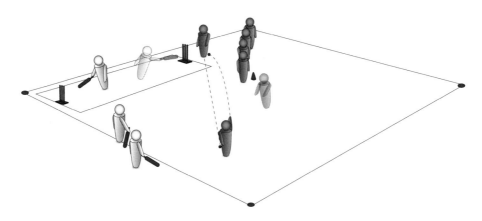

Procedure: Divide groups into two teams, as shown. To begin, a player rolls the ball out in an arc toward the edge of the playing area. As the ball is rolled, two batters attempt to make two runs between the stumps before the first fielder in line runs from the cone behind the bowler, chases the ball, picks it up and throws it back to the bowler. Batters try to score as many runs as they can as the fielders field 10 balls. Teams rotate after an innings so everyone has an opportunity to bat and field. The pair that scores the most runs wins.

Key Points
- When running between the wickets, players make loud, clear calls (Yes! No! Wait!).
- Runners run hard and keep low when approaching the far crease.
- Runners slide the bat over the crease line and face the ball when turning.
- Fielders attack the ball, get low early in a sideways-on position, and maintain balance.
- Fielders keep the head steady and watch the ball, picking it up central to the body with two hands.

Variations: Use a stationary ball; increase or decrease the batter's running area; increase or decrease the fielding area; use a slower or faster serve; use different types of balls.

Batter v Fielder

Objectives: To develop fielding skills and improve running between the wickets; to reduce the number of runs scored when fielding and increase the number of runs scored when running

What You'll Need: Players in groups of 10, 1 tennis ball per group, 3 cones per group, 1 set of stumps per group, at least 1 bat per group

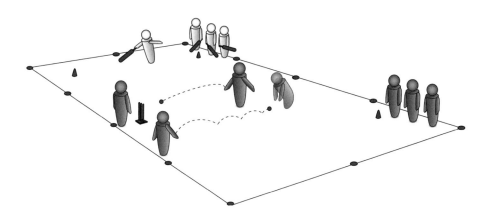

Procedure: Break groups into two teams, as shown. To begin, a player rolls the ball out slowly, and the first player in line for the fielding team attacks the ball and throws underarm at the base of the stumps. At the same time, the first player in line for the batting team runs down the grid to attempt to reach the crease level with the stumps. If the running batter beats the throw, she is awarded 1 point. If the fielding team hits the stumps before the batter reaches the crease, they are awarded 1 point. A set number of repetitions or completion of innings determines the length of the game. The team with the most points overall wins.

Key Points
- When running between wickets, players run hard and reach out with the bat, sliding it over the crease.
- When fielding, players attack the ball and get low early, maintaining balance.
- Fielders watch the ball, picking it up outside of the throwing foot; the throwing hand, arm, and body follow through to the target.

Variations: Increase or decrease running and fielding distances; use different types of balls.

Baseball

Objectives: To develop fielding skills and improve running between the wickets; to reduce the amount of runs scored when fielding and increase the amount of runs scored when running

What You'll Need: 8-12 players, 1 ball per group, 3 sets of stumps per group, 3 cones per group, at least one bat per group

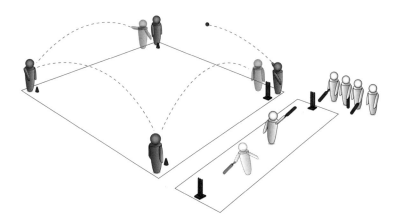

Procedure: Break groups into two teams, as shown. On command, the fielders throw the ball overarm from fielder to fielder around the square, starting and finishing with the player at the stumps. At the same time, the first batter in line runs to the far crease set between the two far cones and back before the ball is returned. If successful, they are awarded two runs; no runs are scored if they do not complete the two runs (down and back); Batters rotate until all are out. Teams swap after a completed innings. The team with the most runs wins.

Key Points

- When running between wickets, players run hard, reach out with the bat, and turn to face the ball.
- Runners keep low when approaching and turning and slide the bat in over the crease lines.
- When throwing, fielders maintain a wide, balanced base.
- When catching, players keep the head steady and watch the ball.
- When catching, the players' hands are together and should "give" with the ball. Fingers point either down or up depending on the type of catch.

Variations: Increase or decrease running or throwing distances; add more players; add another run for the batters; fielders catch one-handed or with the weaker hand; use different types of balls.

Continuous Cricket

Objectives: To acquire and develop batting and fielding skills; to score more runs while batting and only playing at balls that are necessary; to reduce the amount of runs scored when fielding by identifying where batters are hitting the ball; to evaluate and improve execution

What You'll Need: Players in groups of 12, 1 tennis ball per group, 3 cones per group, 1 set of stumps per group, at least 1 bat per group

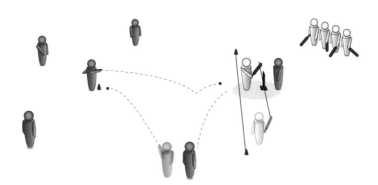

Procedure: Break groups into two teams of six, as shown. To begin, a player acts as the bowler and bowls to the first player in line on the batting team, who attempts to hit the ball. Fielders are no closer than 10 metres (10.9 yards) from the striking batter. Once they have played a shot, batters run around the cones. The bowler can bowl the ball as soon as the fielding side returns the ball. Batters can only be caught or bowled out. Teams swap over when an innings is complete. The team with the most runs wins.

Key Points
- When batting, ensure the grip is correct and that players are in a relaxed, balanced stance.
- Batters watch the ball and apply the correct shot, keeping the ball down.
- When fielding, players react to the ball with hands ready and watch the ball into their hands.
- After fielders secure the ball, they adopt the throwing position and aim at the base of the stumps.
- The fielder backs fielders up to prevent additional runs.

Variations: Hit balls off a cone; use underarm feed, drop feed, or a thrown serve; increase or decrease the size of the fielding area; increase or decrease the size of the running area; increase or decrease the size of the stumps.

Follow the Leader

Objectives: To acquire and develop batting and fielding skills; to score more runs while batting and only playing at balls that are necessary; to reduce the amount of runs scored when fielding by identifying where batters are hitting the ball; to evaluate and improve performance

What You'll Need: Players in groups of 10, 1 tennis ball per group, 7 cones per group, 1 set of stumps per group, 1 bat per group

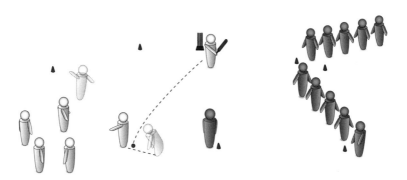

Procedure: Break groups into two teams of five, as shown. A player bowls the ball to the first player in line on the batting team, and this player attempts to hit the ball. The batter and the rest of the batting team form a line and then run around all bases and through the home gate. Once they return to home, the next player in line on the batting team bats. When a ball is hit, the ball is collected by the nearest fielder, and all fielders form a line in the area where it was fielded. The ball is passed along the line, and when it reaches the last player, she throws the ball back to the coach. If the batting team makes it home before the fielding team returns the ball to the coach, they receive 1 point. If the fielding team returns the ball to the coach before the batting team returns home, they receive 1 point. The game is played for a set amount of time. The team with the most points wins.

Key Points

- When batting, ensure the grip is correct and players are in a relaxed, balanced stance.
- Batters watch the ball and apply the correct shot, keeping the ball down.
- When fielding, players react to the ball with hands ready and watch the ball into their hands.
- After fielders secure the ball, they adopt the throwing position and aim at the base of the stumps.
- The fielder backs fielders up to prevent additional runs.

Variations: Increase or decrease the size of the playing area, increase or decrease the number of fielders; batters hit the ball from a tee; vary the types of serves; adjust the scoring; add boundaries.

Round the Cones

Objectives: To acquire and develop batting and fielding skills; to score more runs while batting, playing only at balls that are necessary; to reduce the number of runs scored when fielding; to evaluate and improve execution

What You'll Need: Players in groups of 12, 1 tennis ball per group, 5 cones per group, 1 set of stumps per group, at least one bat per group

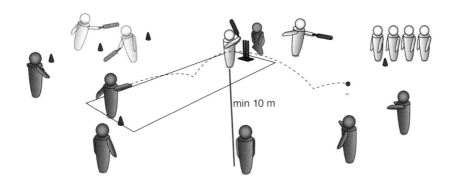

Procedure: Break groups into two teams of six, as shown. The coach feeds the ball to a batter positioned in front of the stumps. The batter attempts to hit the ball and run around the three cones and back to the team. As the first batter reaches the team line, the next batter runs to the crease to hit the next ball. The coach may bowl the next ball as soon as it has been returned by the fielders. One run is scored for every successful completion of the circuit; one run is deducted for a caught or bowled dismissal. Teams rotate when all batters are out or after a set time.

Key Points
- When batting, ensure the grip is correct and that players are in a relaxed, balanced stance.
- Batters watch the ball and apply the correct shot, keeping the ball down.
- When fielding, players react to the ball with hands ready and watch the ball into their hands.
- After fielders secure the ball, they adopt a throwing position and aim at the base of the stumps.
- The fielder backs fielders up to prevent additional runs.

Variations: Increase or decrease boundary size of the playing area, increase or decrease the number of fielders; batters hit the ball from a tee, vary the types of serves; adjust scoring or add boundaries.

Danish Rounders

Objectives: To acquire and develop batting and fielding skills; to score more runs while batting by hitting the ball into gaps and only playing at balls that are necessary; to reduce the amount of runs scored when fielding; to evaluate and improve performance

What You'll Need: Players in groups of 10, 1 tennis ball per group, 4 cones per group, 1 set of stumps per group, at least 1 bat per group

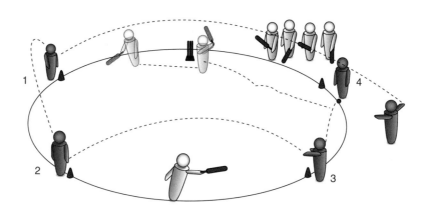

Procedure: Break groups into two teams of five, as shown. The coach serves the ball. Each batter strikes the ball and attempts to run around the cones and back to the baseline. The fielding team retrieves the ball and throws it to each of the bases in turn, attempting to beat the running batter to the final base. There is a fielder on each base and as many (or as few) fielders as needed between the bases. The batting team continues for a set number of time or until all batters are out; teams then rotate. The team that completes the most runs wins.

Key Points
- When batting, ensure the grip is correct and that players are in a relaxed, balanced stance.
- Batters watch the ball and apply the correct shot, keeping the ball down.
- When fielding, players react to the ball with hands ready and watch the ball into their hands.
- After fielders secure the ball, they adopt the throwing position and aim at the base of the stumps.
- The fielder backs fielders up to prevent additional runs.
- Runners run hard and slide the bat over the final baseline in completion.

Variations: Increase or decrease running distance between bases; reduce the number of fielders; add a base; use a bigger ball; use different serves; batters hit the ball from a tee.

About the Author

Ian Pont was a fast-bowling, hard-hitting all-rounder who played first-class cricket for Nottinghamshire and Essex from 1981 to 1988. He was a specialist bowling coach for many professional cricket teams, including Kent, Essex, Worcestershire, and Warwickshire. He has also been a coach involved at the international level with England (2003) and Netherlands (2005-2007) and holds a level 3 UKCC head coach qualification. Ian is currently the Northamptonshire fast bowling consultant. He helped set up and was head coach of the International Cricket Camp in Potchefstroom, South Africa, which takes place each December and features world-class coaches such as Gary Kirsten, Graeme Pollock, and Jimmy Cook. Ian  is widely regarded as the world's leading technical fast bowling coach, having worked with legends Dale Steyn and Darren Gough.

Coaching Youth Sport Series
Ideal for coaches of athletes ages 14 and under

Coaching Youth Basketball 🖱
978-0-7360-6450-7

Coaching Youth Cheerleading 🖱
978-0-7360-7444-5

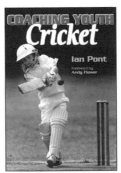
Coaching Youth Cricket
978-0-7360-8370-6

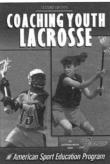
Coaching Youth Lacrosse
978-0-7360-3794-5

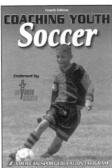
Coaching Youth Soccer 🖱
978-0-7360-6329-6

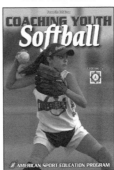
Coaching Youth Softball 🖱
978-0-7360-6258-9

Coaching Youth Tennis 🖱
978-0-7360-6419-4

Coaching Youth Track & Field
978-0-7360-6914-4

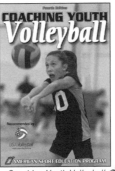
Coaching Youth Volleyball 🖱
978-0-7360-6820-8

Coming Soon!
Coaching Youth Field Hockey
Coaching Youth Gymnastics

ATHLETES FIRST, WINNING SECOND

🖱 Online course also available.

www.ASEP.com

You'll find other outstanding cricket resources at

www.HumanKinetics.com/cricket

In the U.S. call 1-800-747-4457

Australia 08 8372 0999 • Canada 1-800-465-7301
Europe +44 (0) 113 255 5665 • New Zealand 0800 222 062

 HUMAN KINETICS
The Premier Publisher for Sports & Fitness
P.O. Box 5076 • Champaign, IL 61825-5076 USA

 **eBook**
available at
HumanKinetics.com